THE BEST 100 LOVE POEMS
OF THE
SPANISH LANGUAGE

Bilingual Edition

SEABURN PUBLISHING

For information about this anthology write to Seaburn Publishing,
PO Box 2085, Long Island City, NY 11102

The Best 100 Love Poems of the Spanish Language
        [Poems. English & Spanish. Selections]
        Anthology and notes by Pedro Lastra & Rigas Kappatos;
translated by Riga Kappatos, Eleni Paidoussi, Rene de Costa —
Bilingual ed.
English and Spanish
Includes contents and biographical notes.
ISBN 1-885778-40-6 (trade paperback)

Printed in the United States of America

The foundation Vicente Huidobro authorized the
publication of the fragment of "Altazor" of V.
Huidobro; Ms. Doris Dana the two poems of
Gabriela Mistral and the Literary Agency "Carmen
Balcells" the poems of Pablo Neruda. The antholo-
gists express also their gratitude for the authoriza-
tion given to them by the poets or their heirs of
poems subject to copyright.

To Juanita and Gloria

PREFACE

Love is a subject that has rarely failed to inspire poets in all times, in all languages. In the past, wherever there were no written languages, as with the indigenous populations of Latin America, the subject of love was treated within the oral tradition and other forms of art like painting, sculpture...

Love, as Fernando de Herrera said in 1580, is an inexhaustible subject: "Not all thoughts and considerations of love" wrote Herrera in his commentaries on Garcilaso de la Vega, "fell from the spirits of Petrarca, Bembo and the ancients; because it is so varied and extended, and so invigorated in itself, that there are no geniuses who could express it all, thus leaving the possibility to those who follow to complete what they have left out".

The legacy is clear: while there are men and women who feel the arrows of Aphrodite's son, sooner or later they will have to deal with the subject of love, if they are poets.

Love reigns supreme more than any other theme in poetry, and there are as many versions as there are human beings: it is the theme renovating itself ad infinitum.

To write on love demands extreme caution: because it is an essential experience of the human being which involves everybody; it has inspired masterpieces in world poetry; it is also a literary subject that may easily lead to the commonplace and to the ridiculous.

It is universally known that love is "blind" and drives human beings to "insanity"; but it is also known that it inflicts pain and melancholy; it is jubilant exaltations and falls into the "abyss of desperation"; it is violence and it is tenderness, and it is manifested with all its antithetical apparitions as life and death (Eros and Thanatos).

As a theme, love goes back to remote antiquity. According to the cosmogony of Hesiod, the god of Love appeared in third place after Chaos and Gaea, becoming early on a powerful source of inspiration for poets and artists of classical Greece and later Rome. Since its beginning, love is the god one does not make war with because the battle is lost a priori, as the famous verse of Sophocles says: "Love is invincible in battle".

It is not an easy task to select the one hundred best love poems in the literary production of any country. This becomes even more complex and difficult when it involves a selection from a language like Spanish, which is spoken officially in more than twenty countries. The challenge of such a task is, however, stimulating, and since we have assumed it, we would like to explain briefly its motivation and the criteria sustaining it.

This project started in a discussion we had over Gustavo Adolfo Bécquer's famous poem "The Dark Swallows Will Return" which was going to be published in Greek in a bilingual appearance in a literary magazine, addressed to Greek readers. The poems of such a limited selection varied in subject, but the poem of Bécquer led us to think of a selection of the best love poems written in Spanish, something never before done in Greek, and under the limitation of "one hundred."

We both agreed that Bécquer's poem was probably the most well known poem of the Spanish language; it is known not only to writers, artists or literary readers in general, but it is also known to people who don't even know how to read. This is mainly because of its amorous subject which, as we said before, is so important to everyone.

We asked ourselves how we could go about selecting ninety-nine more poems of love, of the same or similar level as the one by Bécquer, matching its artistic and expressive qualities and its communicative efficiency; poems that the memory of readers would receive as familiar voices who spoke to them about their own experience. So it is that the number of "one hundred" represents nothing more than a limit, but with the advantage of a precision which imposes an extremely rigorous selection.

That is how the idea started. In its development we were

guided by our love for poetry in general and the closeness of an entire life in poetry written in Spanish: one, teaching and writing poetry in that language; the other, studying it, selecting personal or collective anthologies of it and translating them into Greek. Before all else, we both cherished our experience as readers, though each with a different degree of participation in the language of Garcilaso, Góngora, Neruda and Mistral.

The production of amorous poetry in Spanish is so extended, that one could easily put together an anthology of the best love poems written in each and every Spanish speaking country (some already exist and are well known, like the volume of amorous poetry in Colombia, entitled "Sentimentario", selected by Darío Jaramillo Agudelo, published in 1987). One can also imagine an anthology of thousands of love poems from all over the Spanish speaking world. Without great difficulty one could also compile such an anthology from the work of only a few poets of the Spanish Golden Age, or with only modernists poets from Latin America, whose love poems, especially sonnets, sound like perfect Apollonian compositions, thanks to their richness and musical harmony, their alliterations and rhymes. Love, nevertheless, has continued and will continue to inspire poets and a special anthology however limited would be partial without the inclusion of contemporary poets.

With this in mind and considering the popularity of Bécquer's poem we thought that there are several dozen poems in the Spanish language that no serious anthologist can ignore in a selection of this kind, although they are vastly known and are often found in school books. They are the most memorable poems. Their omission would lessen the value and reduce the scope of this book. Such is the case, among others, of the dramatic "Nocturne" by Jose Asunción Silva, the intense laments of Garcilaso; the sonnet of the Count of Villamediana to "A lady combing her hair"; of the tragic appeal in the poem of Luis Palés Matos, that Charon allows the poet a little more time with his beloved before taking him away, or the sonnet by Francisco de Terrazas where he compares the woman with a "live building", and Neruda's poem "20" which competes in popularity with Bécquer's poem, and many others.

This concerns the very well known poems that cannot be omitted and which constitute approximately 50% of the book. As for the rest, as with every selection, they express definite aesthetics and preferences, closely shared by both anthologists. Obviously, different anthologists could and would have selected different poems and, in many cases, different poets. We, approximating our knowledge and diminishing our differences, have made an effort to make a selection of the one hundred best love poems of the Spanish language whose strength can be recognized as much by readers of Spanish as by those of the English and Greek languages in various bilingual editions.

To a great extent we believe that we have accomplished our goal. The last word belongs to the reader, who must keep in mind that this is an anthology of poems and not of poets or countries.

Pedro Lastra - Rigas Kappatos

CONTENTS

The anthologists wish to express their thanks to the writer John Kallas for his interest in this project.

JUAN RUIZ, ARCIPRESTE DE HITA

CUALIDADES DE LAS MUJERES CHICAS

Quiero abreviar, señores, la mi predicación,
pues siempre me pagué de pequeño sermón,
y de dueña pequeña y de breve razón,
pues lo poco y bien dicho se hinca en el corazón.

Del que habla mucho, ríen; quien mucho ríe, es loco.
En la mujer pequeña hay amor, y no poco.
Hay muchas dueñas grandes que por chicas "non troco"
pero ambas se arrepienten del cambio que provoco.

Decir bien de las chicas el Amor me hizo ruego
y yo quiero decir sus noblezas muy luego
y hablar de las pequeñas como quien hace juego.
Son frías como nieve, pero arden como el fuego.

Exteriormente frías, con el amor ardientes;
en la cama, solaz: placenteras, rientes,
y en casa, sosegadas, donosas, excelentes.
Tienen mucho de aquello en que tú paras mientes.

En la piedra preciosa yace gran resplandor;
en el trozo de azúcar yace mucho dulzor:
en la dueña pequeña yace enorme el amor.
Pocas palabras bastan al buen entendedor.

Es muy pequeño el grano de la buena pimienta,
pero más que la nuez nos conforta y calienta.
Así dueña pequeña todo amor alimenta.
No hay un placer del mundo que en ella no se sienta.

JUAN RUIZ, ARCHIPRIEST OF HITA
(Spain, ca. 1295 - ca.1353)

CHARMS OF SMALL WOMEN

I wish to make this preaching short,
for a short sermon I always find right,
as I find small women with little brain,
since the few but well expressed words is what counts.

He who talks much is laughed at. He who laughs much
is a fool, for in a little woman there is a lot of love;
that is why I traded lots of big women for little ones.
Although both regret the changes I make.

Love asked me to sing the small ones
and with no delay I will sing their nobility.
I will sing of the small ones playfully.
They are cold like snow, yet burn like fire.

They are cold on the outside, but inside they're burning hot;
they give themselves with joy; they are playful and eager,
at home they have wisdom and respect, first class housewives;
and if you look deeper you will discover they possess a lot
        more grace.

The tiny gem abounds in splendor,
a speck of sugar has great sweetness,
the little woman has great amounts of love,
and for those who understand, it's needless to say more.

A tiny grain of pepper warms the tongue
and is more pleasing to the palate than a walnut:
And a little woman gives much love
and there is no delight that she does not possess.

Tal como en la rosita está intenso el color,
y en partecilla de oro hay gran precio y valor
y en la gota de esencia, la fragancia mayor,
así en la dueña chica se halla todo el sabor.

Como el rubí pequeño tiene mucha bondad,
color, virtud y valor, nobleza y claridad;
así dueña pequeña tiene mucha beldad,
hermosura, donaire, amor y lealtad.

Pequeña es la calandria y chico el ruiseñor,
mas su canto es más dulce que el de otra ave mayor.
La mujer que es pequeña, es por eso mejor.
Enamorada endulza más que azúcar ni flor.

Son aves pequeñitas papagayo y "orior",
pero cualquiera de ellos es dulce gritador.
Vehemente, y hermosa, preciado cantador,
así tal es la dueña pequeña con amor.

De la mujer pequeña ya no hay comparación.
Terrenal paraíso es y gran consolación,
y solaz, y alegría, placer y bendición.
Mejor es en la prueba que en la salutación.

Siempre amé mujer chica más que mujer mayor,
pues no es desaguisado huir de lo peor.
Del mal tomar lo menos, dice el conocedor.
Por tal, de las mujeres, la mejor es la menor.

(Del "Libro de buen amor."
Versión moderna de Clemente Canales Toro)

As a small rose is richly colored
and great value is found in a little piece of gold,
and as a little balsam emits a strong fragrance,
so little women overflow with sweetness.

As the small ruby has much grace and color,
nobility, virtue, clarity and valor,
so the small woman has great beauty,
elegance, love, tenderness and loyalty.

The skylark is a small bird and so is the nightingale,
but larger birds cannot compete in song;
that is why the little woman is more graceful
and in love-making she is sweeter than flowers or honey.

The orioles, the parrots are small birds,
any of them is unique in its singing,
each a graceful, playful little bird, a lovely warbler:
such is the little woman when in love.

The small woman has no comparison:
she is paradise on earth, greatly compassionate,
she is pleasure, enchantment, joy and blessing;
definitely better in actions than in words.

I have always preferred the little to the big or tall.
To try avoiding a calamity, is never a mistake!
Take the lesser of two evils, as the saying goes,
that is why in women the little one is the best.

ANONIMO

FONTE FRIDA, FONTE FRIDA

Fonte frida, fonte frida,   fonte frida y con amor,
do todas las avecicas   van tomar consolación,
si no es la tortolica   qu'está viuda y con dolor;
por allí fuera pasar   el traidor del ruiseñor;
las palabras que le dice   llenas son de traición:
-"Si tú quisieses, señora,   yo sería tu servidor."
-"Vete d'ahí, enemigo,   malo, falso, engañador,
"que ni poso en ramo verde,   ni en prado que tenga flor;
"que si el agua hallo clara   turbia la bebía yo;
"que no quiero haber marido   porque hijos no haya, no;
"no quiero placer con ellos,   ni menos consolación.
"¡Déjame, triste enemigo,   malo, falso, mal traidor,
"que no quiero ser tu amiga   ni casar contigo, no!"

ANONYMOUS

COLD FOUNTAIN, COLD FOUNTAIN

Cold fountain, cold fountain,　refreshing with love,
where all little birds go　to drink consolation,
all but the turtledove　bereaved and in pain;
to that fountain also came　the tricky nightingale;
the words he said to her　were pure trickery:
" If you wish it my lady,　I would become your servant!"
" Go away from my sight,　liar, evil, cheat,
I won't roost on a green bough　nor in a flowering meadow,
if I find clear water　I´d rather drink it cloudy;
I do not want another husband　nor to bear his children, no;
I do not want their joy　nor do I wish for comfort.
Leave me alone you trickster,　liar, fake and evil cheat,
I don't want your friendship　nor do I wish to marry you."

GARCILASO DE LA VEGA

EGLOGA PRIMERA (Fragmentos)

SALICIO
¡Oh más dura que mármol a mis quejas,
y al encendido fuego en que me quemo
más helada que nieve, Galatea!
Estoy muriendo, y aún la vida temo;
témola con razón, pues tú me dejas;
que no hay, sin ti, el vivir para qué sea.
Vergüenza ha que me vea
ninguno en tal estado,
de ti desamparado,
y de mí mismo yo me corro agora.
¿De un alma te desdeñas ser señora
donde siempre moraste, no pudiendo
della salir un hora?
Salid sin duelo, lágrimas, corriendo.
…………………………………………..
Por ti el silencio de la selva umbrosa,
por ti la esquividad y apartamiento
del solitario monte me agradaba;
por ti la verde hierba, el fresco viento,
el blanco lirio y colorada rosa
y dulce primavera deseaba.
¡Ay, cuánto me engañaba!
¡Ah, cuán diferente era
y cuán de otra manera
lo que en tu falso pecho se escondía!
Bien claro con su voz me lo decía
la siniestra corneja repitiendo
la desventura mía.
Salid sin duelo, lágrimas, corriendo.
……………………………………
Tu dulce habla, ¿en cúya oreja suena?
Tus claros ojos, ¿a quién los volviste?
¿Por quién tan sin respeto me trocaste?
Tu quebrantada fe, ¿dó la pusiste?

GARCILASO DE LA VEGA
(Toledo, Spain, 1501 - Nice, France, 1536)

FIRST ECLOGUE (Excerpts)
SALICIO
Oh, to my sobs, Galatea, you are harder than a stone
and to the flames that consume me
you are colder than snow! I am dying
and still I am afraid of life;
it is because you are leaving me;
what good is life without you?
I am afraid that someone
might see me in this state,
abandoned by you,
that I even feel ashamed of myself.
Wasn't it enough for you to be the mistress of a soul
where you always dwelled and reigned, not being able
to stay away from it even for one hour?
Run shamelessly, my tears, run.
....

Because of you the deep silence of the shady forest,
because of you the harshness and desolation
of the lonely mountain that gave me pleasure;
the gentle breeze the tender grass,
the white lily in bloom, the scarlet rose
and the sweet spring I longed for you.
Oh, how wrong I was!
How different
appears
What was hidden in your deceitful chest!
The strange crow told me clearly
echoing
my unhappiness.
Run shamelessly, my tears, run.
....

Whose ear is listening to your sweet words?
Whom are your luminous eyes looking at?
For whom have you so shamelessly abandoned me?
Where do you now lean to rest your shattered faith?

¿Cuál es el cuello que, como en cadena,
de tus hermosos brazos anudaste?
No hay corazón que baste,
aunque fuese de piedra,
viendo mi amada yedra,
de mí arrancada, en otro muro asida,
y mi parra en otro olmo entretejida,
que no se esté con llanto deshaciendo
hasta acabar la vida,
Salid sin duelo, lágrimas , corriendo.
....

Siempre de nueva leche en el verano
y en el invierno abundo; en mi majada
la manteca y el queso está sobrado;
de mi cantar, pues, yo te vi agradada,
tanto, que no pudiera el mantuano
Títiro ser de ti más alabado.
No soy, pues, bien mirado,
tan disforme ni feo;
que aun agora me veo
en esta agua que corre clara y pura;
y cierto no trocara mi figura
con ese que de mí se está riendo;
trocara mi ventura.
Salid sin duelo, lágrimas, corriendo.
....

¿Cómo te vine en tanto menosprecio?
¿Cómo te fui tan presto aborrecible?
¿Cómo te faltó en mí el conocimiento?
Si no tuvieras condición terrible,
siempre fuera tenido de ti en precio,
y no viera de ti este apartamiento.
¿No sabes que sin cuento
buscan en el estío
mis ovejas el frío
de la sierra de Cuenca, y el gobierno
del abrigado Estremo en el invierno?

Whose neck, like a chain's link,
your hands embrace?
There is no heart that can suffer it,
even if made of stone;
to see my beloved ivy,
uprooted from me clinging to another wall;
my vine climbing to another tree,
without melting in endless sobs
until the end of life.
Run shamelessly, my tears, run.
....

Fresh milk in Winter and Summer abounds in my paddock
and there is plenty of cheese and butter;
my song made you happy
so that you could not praise even the Mantuan Titiro
as being better than myself.
After all, I am not unsightful,
neither am I deformed or ugly;
even now as I look at myself in this clear water;
I do not trade this reflection
with the one who now laughs at me.
My destiny, yes, that I would trade.
Run shamelessly, my tears, run.
....
Why this great contempt?
Why this aversion for me in such a short time?
How could you think of me in such a way?
If you were not so terrible,
you would respect me
and I wouldn't have to watch you walk away from me.
You know how my sheep
seek the shade
of the Cuenca mountains in summer
and in the winter
the leeward meadows of Extremadura.

Mas ¿qué vale el tener, si derritiendo
me estoy en llanto eterno?
Salid sin duelo, lágrimas, corriendo.

Con mi llorar las piedras enternecen
su natural dureza y la quebrantan,
los árboles parece que se inclinan;
las aves que me escuchan, cuando cantan,
con diferente voz se condolecen,
y mi morir cantando me adivinan.
Las fieras que reclinan
su cuerpo fatigado
dejan el sosegado
sueño por escuchar mi llanto triste.
Tú sola contra mí te endureciste,
los ojos aun siquiera no volviendo
a lo que tú heciste.
Salid sin duelo, lágrimas, corriendo.
....

NEMOROSO

Corrientes aguas, puras, cristalinas;
árboles que os estáis mirando en ellas,
verde prado de fresca sombra lleno,
aves que aquí sembráis vuestras querellas,
yedra que por los árboles caminas,
torciendo el paso por su verde seno;
yo me vi tan ajeno
del grave mal que siento,
que de puro contento
con vuestra soledad me recreaba,
donde con dulce sueño reposaba,
o con el pensamiento discurría
por donde no hallaba
sino memorias llenas de alegría.
....

But what do all these mean
when I melt in eternal flood of tears?
Run shamelessly, my tears, run.

My wailing moves even the hard stone
shattering its natural rigidity;
the trees look as bending to the ground;
the birds listen to me as they sing,
with a trill that is different
and in their song they prophesy my death.
The wild beasts that rest
their tired bodies,
forget their peaceful sleep
to listen to my lament.
You, alone, have hardened toward me,
and now you do not even look
to see your deed.
Run shamelessly, my tears, run.

....

NEMOROSO
Running waters, crystal clear and pure;
trees there reflected in their stillness,
green meadow of cool shade,
birds lamenting in their song,
ivy scaling on the trees,
wending its way around the green breast;
I felt so estranged
from the grave affliction that engulfs me,
that I basked in your solitude
and the sheer pleasure of it made me happy;
there I relaxed with peaceful sleep,
or traveled in thought
where I found nothing
but happy memories.

....

¿Dó están agora aquellos claros ojos
que llevaban tras sí, como colgada
mi alma doquier que ellos se volvían?
¿Dó está la blanca mano delicada,
llena de vencimientos y despojos
que de mí mis sentidos le ofrecían?
Los cabellos que vían
con gran desprecio el oro,
como a menor tesoro,
¿adónde están?, ¿adónde el blando pecho?
¿Dó la coluna que el dorado techo
con presunción graciosa sostenía?
Aquesto todo agora ya se encierra,
por desventura mía,
en la fría, desierta y dura tierra.
....

Desta manera suelto ya la rienda
a mi dolor, y así me quejo en vano
de la dureza de la muerte airada.
Ella en mi corazón metió la mano,
y de allí me llevó mi dulce prenda;
que aquel era su nido y su morada.
¡Ay muerte arrebatada!
Por ti me estoy quejando
al cielo y enojando
con importuno llanto al mundo todo.
Tan desigual dolor no sufre modo.
No me podrán quitar el dolorido
sentir, si ya del todo
primero no me quitan el sentido.
....

Divina Elisa, pues agora el cielo
con inmortales pies pisas y mides,
y su mudanza ves, estando queda,
¿por qué de mí te olvidas, y no pides
que se apresure el tiempo en que este velo

Where are those sparkling eyes now
that were bringing behind them my soul like hanging,
wherever I glanced?
Where is the cool white hand
replete with spoils and victories
that my senses offered it?
The hair in front of which
gold paled as pleasure
of less worth
where is it? Where is the soft breast?
The proud column
whose grace proudly supported
the golden roof, where is it all now?
Inside the cold, hard, desolate earth
where, for my misfortune, all is now interred.
....

In this way I now unleash the harness of my pain
and mourn in vain
the harsh, merciless death.
Death placed a hand on my heart
and stole my precious gift;
my heart was its house and nest.
Oh, merciless death!
Because of you I raise my grief
to heaven and I anger
with my inopportune lament the whole world.
From such a bottomless pain there is no way out.
No one will ever heal my sorrow;
they would have
to numb my senses first.
....

Divine Elisa, now that you span
the sky with your immortal steps,
and watch its motion transfixed,
why do you forget me?
Why not ask to speed the time when this veil [1]

rompa del cuerpo, y verme libre pueda,
y en la tercera rueda,
contigo mano a mano
busquemos otro llano,
busquemos otros montes y otros ríos,
otros valles floridos y sombríos,
donde descanse, y siempre pueda verte
ante los ojos míos,
sin miedo y sobresalto de perderte?
....

SONETO V

Escrito está en mi alma vuestro gesto
y cuanto yo escribir de vos deseo:
vos sola lo escribistes; yo lo leo
tan solo, que aun de vos me guardo en esto.

En esto estoy y estaré siempre puesto,
que aunque no cabe en mí cuanto en vos veo,
de tanto bien lo que no entiendo creo,
tomando ya la fe por presupuesto.

Yo no nací sino para quereros:
mi alma os ha cortado a su medida;
por hábito del alma misma os quiero;

cuanto tengo confieso yo deberos:
por vos nací, por vos tengo la vida,
por vos he de morir, y por vos muero.

will free me from this veil?
In the third circle then
hand in hand
we will find another plane,
we will find different mountains and other rivers,
other shady and flowered valleys
in which to rest; I will never let you
out of my sight
without the anxiety or the fear of losing you.
....

SONNET V

The image of thee is written in my soul
along with all I want to write about you:
you alone wrote it there, I can only read it
and this I conceal even from thee.

In this I am and in this I shall always be,
though all I see in you cannot fit within me,
such good fortune I cannot fathom yet I believe
for I have my faith to lean on.

I was born only to love thee
my soul is made to fit just you;
and from my soul's want I can love only thee;

whatever I have I owe to thee;
I was born from you, you gave me life,
I'm dying for you; and for you I shall die.

---

[1] In the time of Garcilaso de la Vega, the human body was considered the "veil" (the cover) that contained the soul. Many poets of that period refer to the human body as "veil".

[2] The third circle is the sky of Aphrodite, the light of which is the cause of erotic affairs. No other star equals the power of the beautiful goddess of Love in this matter. All poets of the Spanish Golden Era had extensive knowledge of Greek history, mythology and language. Their poetry makes direct and indirect references to the ancient Greek world and its heroes.

SONETO X

¡Oh dulces prendas por mi mal halladas,
dulces y alegres cuando Dios quería,
juntas estáis en la memoria mía
y con ella en mi muerte conjuradas!

¿Quién me dijera, cuando las pasadas
horas qu'en tanto bien por vos me vía,
que me habíades de ser en algún día
con tan grave dolor representadas?

Pues en una hora junto me llevastes
todo el bien que por términos me distes,
llévame junto al mal que me dejastes;

si no, sospecharé que me pusistes
en tantos bienes, porque deseastes
verme morir entre memorias tristes.

GUTIERRE DE CETINA

MADRIGAL I

Ojos claros, serenos,
si de un dulce mirar sois alabados,
¿por qué, si me miráis, miráis airados?
Si cuanto más piadosos,
más bellos parecéis a aquel que os mira,
no me miréis con ira,
porque no parezcáis menos hermosos.
¡Ay tormentos rabiosos!
Ojos claros, serenos,
ya que así me miráis, miradme al menos.

SONNET X

Oh, sweet gifts brought forth for my misfortune,
sweet and gay as God willed,
you are all now within my memory
and so exorcised you will follow me to my death!

Who could imagine that those hours,
when I was enjoying your divine gifts,
a stormy time would make me pay
with this profound pain I suffer now,

Just as in a short time you took away
all gifts given to me on condition,
oh, take also the pain that I now feel,

otherwise I will surmise that you gave me
those riches so you can see me expire now
because of those sad memories.

GUTIERRE DE CETINA
(Spain, ca.1520 - Mexico, ca.1557)

MADRIGAL I

Luminous, tranquil eyes,
if for the sweetness of your glance you are praised,
why are you angry when you look at me?
If the more chaste you are, the more beautiful you seem
to the one who is looking at you,
don't look at me with such anger,
lest you appear less beautiful.
Oh, angered ordeals!
Luminous, tranquil eyes,
even if you must look at me like that, look at me at least.

ANONIMO

ROMANCE DE AMORES

Si se está mi corazón
en una silla sentado,
circuido de pasión
de firmeza coronado,
tristes de mis pensamientos
que le tenían cercado;
al uno llaman desdicha,
al otro llaman cuidado,
al otro gran desconsuelo,
para mí, desconsolado,
que una señora que sirvo
mis servicios ha olvidado.
Y si yo muero de amores
no me entierren en sagrado,
háganme la sepultura
en un verdecico prado,
y dirán todas las gentes
de qué murió el desdichado:
no murió de calentura
ni de dolor de costado,
mas murió de mal de amores
que es un mal desesperado.

(Del "Cancionero llamado Flor de enamorados")

ANONYMOUS

ROMANCE OF LOVE

When my heart settles
comfortably into a seat,
surrounded by passion,
fixed by sad thoughts
that engulf it.
One is called misfortune,
the other is called concern,
and yet another
is despair
the next despair,
woe to me so unfortunate,
for a lady whom I have served
has forgotten my services.
If I die of love
do not bury me in a hallowed ground,
bury me instead
in a green meadow,
where people will ask:
what did this unlucky one die from?
He did not die of fever
nor of a pain in his ribs;
he died of love
which is a terminal disease.

FRANCISCO DE TERRAZAS

A UNA DAMA

Dejad las hebras de oro ensortijado
que el ánima me tienen enlazada,
y volved a la nieve no pisada
lo blanco de esas rosas matizado.

Dejad las perlas y el coral preciado
de que esa boca está tan adornada;
y al cielo, de quien sois tan envidiada,
volved los soles que le habéis robado.

La gracia y discreción que muestra ha sido
del gran saber del celestial maestro,
volvédselo a la angélica natura;

y todo aquesto así restituido
veréis que lo que os queda es propio vuestro:
ser áspera, cruel, ingrata y dura.

FRANCISCO DE TERRAZAS
(Mexico, 1525 - 1560) ,(Nueva España)

TO A LADY

Away with the curly, golden hair
that has my soul entwined
and give back to the unspoiled snow
tinting its whiteness with these roses.

Away with the pearls, the precious coral
that graces your mouth; and to the sky,
that envies you so much for this,
return the sun that you have stolen.

Your grace and carriage, unshaken proof
of the great wisdom of the heavenly master,
return them to the angels. When all this is done

and all is returned to universal law,
you will see then that what remains is you alone:
harsh, cruel, ungrateful, made of stone.

A UNAS PIERNAS

¡Ay basas de marfil, vivo edificio
obrado del artífice del cielo,
columnas de alabastro que en el suelo
nos dais del bien supremo claro indicio!

¡Hermosos capiteles y artificio
del arco que aun de mí me pone celo!
¡Altar donde el tirano dios mozuelo
hiciera de sí mismo sacrificio!

¡Ay puerta de la gloria de Cupido
y guarda de la flor más estimada
de cuantas en el mundo son ni han sido!

Sepamos hasta cuándo estáis cerrada
y el cristalino cielo es defendido
a quien jamás gustó fruta vedada.

TO A PAIR OF LEGS

Oh, pedestals of ivory, breathing structure,
labor of a master's heavenly hand,
columns of alabaster giving us
authentic evidence of a divine product!

Fair capitals, arches of such craftsmanship
that arouse me so!
Altar where the tyrannical little God
would sacrifice himself!

Oh, triumphant arch of Eros,
guardian of the most precious flower,
that ever did exist or will exist on earth!

Let us know how long you'll be closed
and the crystal sky will remain banned
to one who has never yearned for forbidden fruit.

FERNANDO DE HERRERA

SONETO XXXII

¡Oh cara perdición, oh dulce engaño,
suave mal, sabroso descontento,
amado error del tierno pensamiento,
luz que nunca descubre el desengaño!

Puerta por la cual entra el bien y el daño,
descanso y pena grave del tormento,
vida del mal, alma del sufrimiento,
de confusión revuelta cerco extraño,

vario mar de tormenta y de bonanza,
segura playa y peligroso puerto,
sereno, instable, oscuro y claro cielo:

¿por qué, como me diste confianza
d'osar perderme, ya qu'estoy desierto
de bien, no pones a mi mal consuelo?

FERNANDO DE HERRERA
(Spain, 1534 - 1597)

SONNET XXXII

Oh, dearest loss, sweet illusion;
gentle evil, delightful discontent,
beloved error of a tender thought,
light which never reveals the fraud!

Door through which both good and evil enter,
restfulness and grave pain of tyranny,
life of evils, soul of martyrdom,
strange cycle of reversed confusion,

unstable sea of roughness and calm,
secure sea-shore and risky port,
clear, unstable sky of darkness:

why since you made hazard my loss,
now that good has already left me desolate
won't you cure this evil with consolation?

FRANCISCO DE ALDANA

SONETO XII

"¿Cuál es la causa, mi Damón, que estando
en la lucha de amor juntos trabados
con lenguas, brazos, pies y encadenados
cual vid que entre el jazmín se va enredando

"y que el vital aliento ambos tomando
en nuestros labios, de chupar cansados,
en medio a tanto bien somos forzados
llorar y suspirar de cuando en cuando?"

"Amor, mi Filis bella, que allá dentro
nuestras almas juntó, quiere en su fragua
los cuerpos ajuntar también tan fuerte

"que no pudiendo, como esponja el agua,
pasar del alma al dulce amado centro
llora el velo mortal su avara suerte."

FRANCISCO DE ALDANA
(Spain, 1537 - Morocco, 1578)

SONNET XII

"Which is the reason my Damon that although
we are tied up in love's struggle
with tongues, hands, feet, braided
like a vine on the jasmine plant,

that the two of us take breath of life
in our lips, to drink exhausted
by all these riches, why are we forced
by nature to sigh and cry more often than not?"

"Eros, my beautiful Filis, that has united
our souls, now in the workshop wishes to
unite our bodies as well, perfectly, fully

and not being able to pass, like a sponge the water,
from the soul to the sweet, beloved center,
bemoans its niggardly fate, the mortal veil[1]".

[1] Veil= body

LUIS DE GONGORA Y ARGOTE

SONETO LXXXII

La dulce boca que a gustar convida
un humor entre perlas distilado,
y a no invidiar aquel licor sagrado
que a Júpiter ministra el garzón de Ida,

amantes, no toquéis, si queréis vida;
porque entre un labio y otro colorado
Amor está, de su veneno armado,
cual entre flor y flor sierpe escondida.

No os engañen las rosas, que a la Aurora
diréis que, aljofaradas y olorosas,
se le cayeron del purpúreo seno;

manzanas son de Tántalo, y no rosas,
que después huyen del que incitan ahora,
y sólo del Amor queda el veneno.

LUIS DE GONGORA Y ARGOTE
(Spain, 1561 - 1627)

SONNET LXXXII

The sweet mouth that offers for a taste
a breath distilled in pearls;
do not envy, lovers, the ambrosia
which Zeus is offered by Ganymede,

do not touch it if you wish to live,
for between those coral lips
Eros awaits armed with poison,
like a snake in wait amongst the flowers.

Don't be deceived by the roses
perfumed and pearl embroidered that look as if
they dropped from Dawn's bright red bosom;

they are not roses, but Tantalus' apples;
that move away from the one they torture
and what remains is only Love's poison.

SONETO CIII

*De un caminante enfermo que se enamoró donde fue
hospedado*

Descaminado, enfermo, peregrino,
en tenebrosa noche, con pie incierto
la confusión pisando del desierto,
voces en vano dio, pasos sin tino.

Repetido latir, si no vecino,
distinto, oyó de can siempre despierto,
y en pastoral albergue mal cubierto,
piedad halló, si no halló camino.

Salió el Sol, y entre armiños escondida,
soñolienta beldad con dulce saña
salteó al no bien sano pasajero.

Pagará el hospedaje con la vida;
más le valiera errar en la montaña
que morir de la suerte que yo muero.

SONNET CIII

About a sick traveler who fell in love where he found
hospitality

A sick, lost traveler, wandering in the mists of night
with uncertain steps,
staggers on the confusion of the desert;
screaming in vain he walked randomly.

He heard the distant barking
of an ever alert watch dog.
It led him to a half wrecked pen
where he finds not his way, but hospitality.

At sunrise, bundled in ermine,
a sleepy-eyed beauty, adroitly
leapt suddenly in front of the sick traveler.

He will pay the hospitality with his life;
it would've been best to be lost in the mountains,
rather than die from what I'm dying now.

LOPE DE VEGA Y CARPIO

SONETO LXI

Ir y quedarse, y con quedar partirse,
partir sin alma, y ir con alma ajena,
oír la dulce voz de una sirena
y no poder del árbol desasirse;

arder como la vela y consumirse,
haciendo torres sobre tierna arena,
caer de un cielo, y ser demonio en pena,
y de serlo jamás arrepentirse;

hablar entre las mudas soledades;
pedir prestada sobre fe paciencia,
y lo que es temporal llamar eterno;

creer sospechas y negar verdades,
es lo que llaman en el mundo ausencia,
fuego en el alma, y en la vida infierno.

LOPE DE VEGA Y CARPIO
(Spain, 1562-1635)

SONNET LXI

To leave yet to stay, and by staying to leave
one's soul behind; and leave with the soul of another
to listen to the sweet voice of a siren
unable to loosen oneself from the mast;

to burn like a candle, to melt,
building castles in the soft sand,
to fall from heaven to earth,
desperate but without remorse;

to talk to yourself in the mute solitudes;
to seek patience by pledging your faith,
and to call the temporal eternal;

to believe suspicions and deny truths,
is what the world calls absence,
fire in the soul and life in hell.

SONETO CLXXXVIII

Suelta mi manso, mayoral extraño,
pues otro tienes de tu igual decoro,
deja la prenda que en el alma adoro,
perdida por tu bien y por mi daño.

Ponle su esquila de labrado estaño,
y no le engañen tus collares de oro,
toma en albricias este blanco toro,
que a las primeras hierbas cumple un año.

Si pides señas, tiene el vellocino
pardo encrespado, y los ojuelos tiene
como durmiendo en regalado sueño.

Si piensas que no soy su dueño, Alcino,
suelta, y verásle si a mi choza viene,
que aún tienen sal las manos de su dueño.

SONNET CLXXXVIII

Untie my fatted lamb strange shepherd,
you possess one from your own class;
the adored pawn, my loss, that has become your fortune,
untie it, let it come to my pen.

Hang a bell of hammered pewter on its neck,
you cannot deceive it with your gold necklaces,
as an exchange take this white bull;
it will be one year old with the new grass.

Its hair is brown and curly, if you are looking
for signs, and its eyes are misty
as if just out of sweet sleep.

If, Alcinoüs, you don't believe I am its owner,
let it loose and you'll see that it will run to my pen,
where his master's hands still hold salt.

FRANCISCO DE MEDRANO

SONETO XLI

Quien te dice que ausencia causa olvido
mal supo amar, porque si amar supiera,
¿qué, la ausencia?: la muerte nunca hubiera
las mientes de su amor adormecido.

¿Podrá olvidar su llaga un corzo herido
del acertado hierro, cuando quiera
huir medroso, con veloz carrera,
las manos que la flecha han despedido?

Herida es el amor tan penetrante
que llega al alma; y tuya fue la flecha
de quien la mía dichosa fue herida.

No temas, pues, en verme así distante,
que la herida, Amarili, una vez hecha,
siempre, siempre y doquiera, será herida.

FRANCISCO DE MEDRANO
(Spain, 1570-1607)

SONNET XLI

He who believes that absence
breeds oblivion, has never truly loved,
for if he loved, what absence! even death
would never be able to erase his thoughts of love.

How can a deer ever forget the wound
from the iron that found its mark, when terrified
it only wants to run swiftly away
from those hands that launched the flying arrow.

Love is a wound so deep it reaches
into the soul; it was your arrow
that gave my heart the wound of happiness.

Do not fear, then, Amarylis, when
You see me distant; the wound that love inflicts
wherever that may be, will always be a wound.

FRANCISCO DE QUEVEDO Y VILLEGAS

SONETO AMOROSO DIFINIENDO EL AMOR

Es hielo abrasador, es fuego helado,
es herida que duele y no se siente,
es un soñado bien, un mal presente,
es un breve descanso muy cansado.

Es un descuido que nos da cuidado.
Un cobarde, con nombre de valiente,
un andar solitario entre la gente,
un amar solamente ser amado.

Es una libertad encarcelada,
que dura hasta el postrero parasismo;
enfermedad que crece si es curada.

Este es el niño Amor, éste es su abismo.
¡Mirad cuál amistad tendrá con nada
el que en todo es contrario de sí mismo!

FRANCISCO DE QUEVEDO Y VILLEGAS
(Spain, 1580-1645)

AMOROUS SONNET DEFINING LOVE

It is burning ice, it is a cold fire,
it is a wound that hurts but you don't feel it,
it is an ideal virtue, an ominous experience of the now,
it is a brief and tired repose.

It is a carelessness which creates concern,
a coward going by a valiant name,
a solitary walk among the multitudes,
a self-complacent love that seeks only to be loved.

It is a freedom in chains
which lasts to the last madness;
a sickness that spreads as it heals.

This is the winged Eros, the magic of its abyss.
How can he be friends with anyone
when he is antagonistic to himself?

AMOR CONSTANTE MAS ALLA DE LA MUERTE

Cerrar podrá mis ojos la postrera
sombra que me llevare el blanco día,
y podrá desatar esta alma mía
hora a su afán ansioso lisonjera;

mas no, de esotra parte, en la ribera,
dejará la memoria, en donde ardía:
nadar sabe mi llama la agua fría,
y perder el respeto a ley severa.

Alma a quien todo un dios prisión ha sido,
venas que humor a tanto fuego han dado,
medulas que han gloriosamente ardido,

su cuerpo dejará, no su cuidado;
serán ceniza, mas tendrá sentido;
polvo serán, mas polvo enamorado.

LOVE BEYOND DEATH

My eyes can be closed by the last shadow
the white day[1] will bring
and take my soul to the sunset; this soul
that now lives in this affected agony;

but not that other part, in the river bank, [2]
that will abandon memory, where it was burning:
in the cold water my flame knows how
to swim, and disregard severe laws.

A soul that has imprisoned a great God, [3]
veins that gave the breath of life to so much fire,
marrows that burned in glory with it

will leave its body, but not its care, [4]
everything will be ashes, but ashes with feeling;
dust they will be, but dust in love.

[1] Death
[2] River Acheron
[3] Eros
[4] Its memory

PROSIGUE EN EL MISMO ESTADO DE SUS AFECTOS

Amor me ocupa el seso y los sentidos;
absorto estoy en éxtasi amoroso;
no me concede tregua ni reposo
esta guerra civil de los nacidos.

Explayóse el raudal de mis gemidos
por el grande distrito doloroso
del corazón, en su penar dichoso,
y mis memorias anegó en olvidos.

Todo soy ruinas, todo soy destrozos,
escándalo funesto a los amantes,
que fabrican de lástimas sus gozos.

Los que han de ser, y los que fueron antes,
estudien su salud en mis sollozos,
y envidien mi dolor, si son constantes.

CONTINUES IN THE SAME STATE OF FEELING

Love holds my thoughts and feelings.
I am submerged in an amorous ecstasy,
this civil war of mortals accepts no talks
of armistice or truce and I am done in.

The cataract was silenced by my sighs
and the depth of pain in my heart,
that is the happiness of punishment and my pains
and drowned even my memories in oblivion.

I am devastated, completely defeated,
a sad sight for those in love,
who build their joy on sorrow.

Those yet to come and those who are no more,
should study their health in my sobs,
and if they have the heart, let them envy my pain.

JUAN DE TASSIS PERALTA, CONDE DE VILLAMEDIANA

A UNA DAMA QUE SE PEINABA

En ondas de los mares no surcados
navecilla de plata dividía,
una cándida mano la regía
con viento de suspiros y cuidados.

Los hilos que de frutos separados
el abundancia pródiga esparcía,
dellos avaro Amor los recogía,
dulce prisión forzando a sus forzados.

Por este mismo proceloso Egeo,
con naufragio feliz va navegando
mi corazón cuyo peligro adoro.

Y las velas al viento desplegando,
rico en la tempestad halla el deseo
escollo de diamante en golfos de oro.

JUAN DE TASSIS PERALTA, COUNT OF VILLAMEDIANA
(Spain, 1582-1622)

TO A LADY COMBING HER HAIR

In waves of untraveled seas
a little silver boat was dividing,
guided by a candid hand
with winds of sighs and cares.

The fibers of divided fruit
scattered the prodigious abundance,
while avaricious Love was collecting them,
and locking them in a delightful prison.

In this same storm-thrashed Aegean Sea,
in a merry shipwreck my heart travels,
whose dangers I adore.

And when the sails open to the winds,
there is rich realization in the tormented waters:
a diamond reef in golden bays.

AMOR NO ES VOLUNTAD, SINO DESTINO

Amor no es voluntad, sino destino
de violenta pasión y fe con ella;
elección nos parece y es estrella
que sólo alumbra el propio desatino.

Milagro humano en símbolos divino,
ley que sus mismas leyes atropella;
ciega deidad, idólatra querella,
que da fin y no medio a su camino.

Sin esperanza, y casi sin deseo,
recatado del propio pensamiento,
en ansias vivas acabar me veo.

Persuasión eficaz de mi tormento,
que parezca locura y devaneo
lo que es amor, lo que es conocimiento.

LOVE IS NOT WILL BUT DESTINY

Love is not will, it is fate
of violent passion and blind faith in it.
It seems that we choose it but it's the star
which orients its own madness.

A human miracle with divine symbols
a law that breaks its own rules,
a blind deity, an idolatrous quarrel,
whose course is the end, not the means.

Without hope and almost without desire,
hiding from my own thought,
I see my end coming filled with agonies.

It is sufficient persuasion of my torment,
that looks like delirium and madness
that which is love, that which is knowledge.

SOR JUANA INES DE LA CRUZ

QUE CONTIENE UNA FANTASIA CONTENTA CON
AMOR DECENTE

Detente, sombra de mi bien esquivo,
imagen del hechizo que más quiero,
bella ilusión por quien alegre muero,
dulce ficción por quien penosa vivo.

Si al imán de tus gracias, atractivo,
sirve mi pecho de obediente acero,
¿para qué me enamoras lisonjero
si has de burlarme luego fugitivo?

Mas blasonar no puedes, satisfecho,
de que triunfa de mí tu tiranía:
que aunque dejas burlado el lazo estrecho

que tu forma fantástica ceñía,
poco importa burlar brazos y pecho
si te labra prisión mi fantasía.

SOR JUANA INES DE LA CRUZ
(Mexico, 1651-1695)

IN CONTAINING A THOUGHT SATISFIED WITH CHASTE LOVE

Stop, shadow of my tricky fate,
image of the magic I love most,
chimera for whom I'd happily die,
sweet myth for whom I live in pain.

If attracted to the magnet of your grace,
can serve my chest of obedient steel,
why do you flirt with me frivolously,
since you will trick me and later leave?

You will not gloat that your tyranny triumphs.
No, you will not boast of that in your life,
though you mock and leave the tight bond

that holds me to your fantastic figure,
it matters little if you trick my body
since I forge you a prison in my fantasy.

EN QUE SATISFACE UN RECELO CON LA RETORICA DEL LLANTO

Esta tarde, mi bien, cuando te hablaba,
como en tu rostro y tus acciones vía
que con palabras no te persuadía,
que el corazón me vieses deseaba;

y Amor, que mis intentos ayudaba,
venció lo que imposible parecía:
pues entre el llanto, que el dolor vertía,
el corazón deshecho destilaba.

Baste ya de rigores, mi bien, baste;
no te atormenten más celos tiranos
ni el vil recelo tu quietud contraste

con sombras necias, con indicios vanos,
pues ya en líquido humor viste y tocaste
mi corazón deshecho entre tus manos.

THE PLEASURE GIVEN BY SUSPICION WITH THE RHETORIC OF CRYING

This afternoon, my treasure, when I talked with you
I saw in your face and movements
that I would not persuade you with words
to look deep into my heart is what I most wished for.

Love, helping my intentions,
did what seemed impossible:
my heart was melting in tears
that the pain brought on.

Enough with sternness my love, enough;
stop bleeding from tyrannical jealousies,
do not let suspicions disturb your serenity

with troublesome shadows and worthless sighs,
since you have seen and touched in damp breath
my lacerated heart in your two hands.

MANUEL DE NAVARRETE

LA SEPARACION DE CLORILA

Luego que de la noche el negro velo
por la espaciosa selva se ha extendido,
parece que de luto se han vestido
las bellas flores del ameno suelo.

Callan las aves, y con tardo vuelo
cada cual se retira al dulce nido.
¡Qué silencio en el valle se ha esparcido!
Todo suscita un triste desconsuelo.

Sólo del búho se oye el ronco acento;
de la lechuza el eco quebrantado,
y el medroso ladrar del can hambriento.

Queda el mundo en tristeza sepultado,
como mi corazón en el momento
que se aparta Clorila de mi lado.

(De "Entretenimientos poéticos")

MANUEL DE NAVARRETE
(Mexico, 1768-1809)

THE SEPARATION FROM CLORILA

After the night's black veil
spread over the immense forest,
the splendid flowers of the happy ground
look as if they were clad in mourning.

The birds, silent, flight delayed
speed to the sweet nest.
What silence reigns in the valley!
A sad despair covers all.

Only the hoarse cry of the owl,
the broken echo of the night bird
and the fearful barking of a hungry dog

are heard. The world is buried in sorrow,
as was my heart when the time came
for Clorila to leave my side.

GERTRUDIS GOMEZ DE AVELLANEDA

IMITANDO UNA ODA DE SAFO

¡Feliz quien junto a ti por ti suspira,
quien oye el eco de tu voz sonora,
quien el halago de tu risa adora,
y el blando aroma de tu aliento aspira!

Ventura tanta, que envidioso admira
el querubín que en el empíreo mora,
el alma turba, al corazón devora,
y el torpe acento, al expresarla, expira.

Ante mis ojos desparece el mundo,
y por mis venas circular ligero
el fuego siento del amor profundo.

Trémula, en vano resistirte quiero…
De ardiente llanto mi mejilla inundo…
¡delirio, gozo, te bendigo y muero!

GERTRUDIS GOMEZ DE AVELLANEDA
(Cuba, 1814 - Spain, 1873)

IMITATING AN ODE BY SAPHO

Happy the one who sighs for you by your side,
who hears the echo of your musical voice,
who adores the flattery of your laughter,
and breathes the soft aroma of your breath!

Such good fortune envied and admired
by the cherub who dwells in heaven,
troubles the soul and sinks the heart,
and the awkward accent, by expressing it, expires.

The world vanishes in front of my eyes
and in my veins I feel deeply love's fire
flow gently inside of me.

Trembling, in vain I try to resist you...
with warm tears I drench my cheeks...
Delirium, delight, I bless you and I die!

GUSTAVO ADOLFO BECQUER

VOLVERAN LAS OSCURAS GOLONDRINAS

Volverán las oscuras golondrinas
en tu balcón sus nidos a colgar,
y otra vez con el ala a sus cristales
    jugando, llamarán;
pero aquellas que el vuelo refrenaban
tu hermosura y mi dicha al contemplar,
aquellas que aprendieron nuestros nombres,
    esas.... ¡no volverán!

Volverán las tupidas madreselvas
de tu jardín las tapias a escalar,
y otra vez a la tarde, aún más hermosas,
    sus flores se abrirán;
pero aquellas cuajadas de rocío,
cuyas gotas mirábamos temblar
y caer, como lágrimas del día...
    esas... ¡no volverán!

Volverán del amor en tus oídos
las palabras ardientes a sonar;
tu corazón de su profundo sueño
    tal vez despertará;
pero mudo y absorto y de rodillas,
como se adora a Dios ante su altar,
como yo te he querido... desengáñate,
    ¡así no te querrán!

GUSTAVO ADOLFO BECQUER
(Spain, 1836-1870)

THE BLACK SWALLOWS WILL RETURN

The black swallows will return
to build their nests on your balcony,
again with their wings on your window
  in their play they will knock;
but those who refrained their flight
to contemplate your beauty and my luck,
those who had learned our names,
  those...will not return!

The dense honeysuckles will return
to climb your garden walls again,
and again in the afternoon, even more beautiful,
  their flowers will bloom;
but the ones solid with frost,
whose trembling drops we watched fall,
like the tears shed by the day...
  those...will not return!

The fiery words of love will return
to echo in your ears again;
maybe your heart from its deep sleep
  will once more awake;
but silent, kneeling, thoughtful,
as one worships God in his shrine,
as I have loved you...don't be deluded,
  no one will ever love you so!

JOSE MARTI

IX

Quiero, a la sombra de un ala,
Contar este cuento en flor:
La niña de Guatemala,
La que se murió de amor.

Eran de lirios los ramos,
Y las orlas de reseda
Y de jazmín: la enterramos
En una caja de seda.

…Ella dio al desmemoriado
Una almohadilla de olor;
El volvió, volvió casado:
Ella se murió de amor.

Iban cargándola en andas
Obispos y embajadores;
Detrás iba el pueblo en tandas,
Todo cargado de flores.

…Ella, por volverlo a ver,
Salió a verlo al mirador;
El volvió con su mujer:
Ella se murió de amor.

Como de bronce candente
Al beso de despedida
Era su frente ¡la frente
Que más he amado en mi vida!

…Se entró de tarde en el río,
La sacó muerta el doctor:
Dicen que murió de frío:
Yo sé que murió de amor.

JOSE MARTI
(Cuba, 1853-1895)

IX

I want, in the shade of a wing,
To tell this story
Of the girl from Guatemala,
Whom love has killed.

The bouquets were of lilies,
The borders were of resedas
And jasmines: we buried her
In a silken coffin.

She left to the forgetful one
A scented little pad:
He returned, but he was married;
She died of love.

She was carried on a bier
By ambassadors and bishops;
Behind followed the crowds,
All replete with flowers.

She, to catch one more glimpse of him,
Came out on the balcony;
He was with his wife:
She died of love.

Like incandescent bronze
In the farewell kiss
Was her forehead. That forehead
That I most loved in life!

One afternoon she waded into the river,
She was taken out dead:
They say she died of cold:
I know she died of love.

Allí, en la bóveda helada,
La pusieron en dos bancos:
Besé su mano afilada,
Besé sus zapatos blancos.

Callado, al oscurecer,
Me llamó el enterrador:
¡Nunca más he vuelto a ver
A la que murió de amor!

(De "Versos sencillos")

There, in her cold crypt,
They placed her across two pews:
I kissed her slender hand,
I kissed her white shoes.

Silent, when night fell,
The grave-digger called me:
I never saw again
The one who died of love.

MANUEL GUTIERREZ NAJERA

NON OMNIS MORIAR

¡No moriré del todo, amiga mía!
De mi ondulante espíritu disperso,
algo en la urna diáfana del verso,
piadosa guardará la poesía.

¡No moriré del todo! Cuando herido
caiga a los golpes del dolor humano,
ligera tú, del campo entenebrido
levantarás al moribundo hermano.

Tal vez entonces por la boca inerme
que muda aspira la infinita calma,
oigas la voz de todo lo que duerme
¡con los ojos abiertos en mi alma!

Hondos recuerdos de fugaces días,
ternezas tristes que suspiran solas:
pálidas, enfermizas alegrías,
sollozando al compás de las violas..

Todo lo que medroso oculta el hombre
se escapará, vibrante, del poeta,
en áureo ritmo de oración secreta
que invoque en cada cláusula tu nombre.

Y acaso adviertas que de modo extraño
suenan mis versos en tu oído atento,
y en el cristal, que con mi soplo empaño,
mires aparecer mi pensamiento.

Al ver entonces lo que yo soñaba,
dirás de mi errabunda poesía:
era triste, vulgar lo que cantaba…
¡mas, qué canción tan bella la que oía!

MANUEL GUTIERREZ NAJERA
(Mexico, 1859-1895)

NON OMNIS MORIAR

I will not die completely, my dear friend!
From my ondulating, spread spirit,
poetry, pious, will treasure something
in the transparent urn of love.

I will not die completely! When I fall
wounded by the blows of human pain,
you, light-footed, will rescue the dying brother
from the dark battlefield.

Maybe then, from my defenseless mouth
that will be breathing the infinite peace silently,
you may hear the voice of all who sleep
with wide-open eyes in my soul!

Profound memories of fleeting days,
sad, tender moments that sigh alone:
pale, sickly joys crying
with sobs accompanied by violas...

Everything that timid men hide
will spring vibrant from the poet
in the golden rhythm of a secret prayer,
that mentions your name with every phrase.

Maybe then you'll see how strange
my verses sound in your ears,
and in the windowpane, which my breath will cloud,
you'll see my most innermost thoughts emerging.

To see then what I dreamed,
you will say of my wandering poetry:
it was sad and vulgar what he sang...
but what a beatiful song the one I was hearing!

Y porque alzo en tu recuerdo notas
del coro universal, vívido y almo;
y porque brillan lágrimas ignotas
en el amargo cáliz de mi salmo;

porque existe la Santa Poesía
y en ella irradias tú, mientras disperso
átomo de mi ser esconda el verso,
¡no morirè del todo, amiga mía!

(De "Poesías")

And because I raise in your memory
a universal choir, vivid, sacred;
because your tears shine unexplored
in the bitter chalice of my psalm;

because the Holy Poetry exists
and you shine in it, while dispersed
atoms of me are hidden in the verse,
I will not die completely, my dear!

JULIAN DEL CASAL

MIS AMORES

Amo el bronce, el cristal, las porcelanas
las vidrieras de múltiples colores,
los tapices pintados de oro y flores
y las brillantes lunas venecianas.

Amo también las bellas castellanas,
la canción de los viejos trovadores,
los árabes corceles voladores,
las flébiles baladas alemanas.

Pero amo mucho más, Rosa hechicera,
que escuchas mis cantares amorosos,
contemplar con miradas devorantes,

el oro de tu larga cabellera,
el rojo de tus labios temblorosos,
y el negro de tus ojos centelleantes.

(De "Hojas al viento")

JULIAN DEL CASAL
(Cuba, 1863-1893)

MY LOVES

I love the bronze, the crystal and the porcelains,
the stained glass windows with their many colors,
the tapestries of gold and flowers
and the brilliant Venetian mirrors.

I also love the beauties of Castille,
the songs of the ancient troubadours,
the swift Arabian horses in their flight,
and the sad German ballads.

But most of all, enchantress Rose,
you who listen to my song of love;
I love to look and drink you in with my eyes,

the gold of your long hair,
the red of your trembling lips,
and the blackness of your sparkling eyes.

JOSE ASUNCION SILVA

NOCTURNO

Una noche,
Una noche toda llena de perfumes, de murmullos y de músicas
    de alas;
    Una noche
En que ardían en la sombra nupcial y húmeda, las luciérnagas
    fantásticas,
A mi lado, lentamente, contra mí ceñida, toda,
    Muda y pálida
Como si un presentimiento de amarguras infinitas
Hasta el fondo más secreto de tus fibras te agitara,
Por la senda que atraviesa la llanura florecida
    Caminabas;
    Y la luna llena
Por los cielos azulosos, infinitos y profundos, esparcía su luz
    blanca,
    Y tu sombra
    Fina y lánguida,
    Y mi sombra
Por los rayos de la luna proyectada
Sobre las arenas tristes
De la senda se juntaban *en algún punto*
    Y eran una
    Y eran una
Y eran una sola sombra larga!
Y eran una sola sombra larga!
Y eran una sola sombra larga!
    Esta noche
    Solo, el alma
Llena de las infinitas amarguras y agonías de tu muerte,
Separado de ti misma, por la sombra, por el tiempo y la
    distancia,
    Por el infinito negro,
    Donde nuestra voz no alcanza,
    Solo y mudo
    Por la senda caminaba,

no doubt that it's about his sister

JOSE ASUNCION SILVA
(Colombia, 1865- 1896)

NOCTURNE   *walking together*

One night,
One night full of perfumes, music of wings and murmurs
One night
When in the nuptial shadow the fantasy fireflies were blazing,
At my side, slowly, glued to me, all of you,
Pale and silent
As if an ill omen of infinite sorrows
Were shaking you to the innermost depths of your being,
You were walking on the path crossing the valley
In bloom;
And the full moon
Spread its light in the deep, azure and endless heavens,
And your shadow
Slim and languid,
And my shadow,
That the moon rays were casting
On the sad sand
Of the path were united
And they were one
And they were one
And there was only one long shadow!
And there was only one long shadow!
And there was one and only one long shadow!
Tonight
All alone,
And my soul full of the sorrows of your death,
Separated from you, from your shadow, from time and
distance,
In the endless blackness,
Where our voice cannot be heard,
Alone and silent
I was walking on the path,

Y se oían los ladridos de los perros a la luna,
    A la luna pálida
    Y el chillido
    De las ranas.
¡Sentí frío, era el frío que tenían en la alcoba
Tus mejillas y tus sienes y tus manos adoradas,
    Entre las blancuras níveas
    De las mortuorias sábanas!
Era el frío del sepulcro, era el frío de la muerte,
    era el frío de la nada...
    Y mi sombra
    Por los rayos de la luna proyectada,
    Iba sola,
    Iba sola
    ¡Iba sola por la estepa solitaria!
    Y tu sombra esbelta y ágil,
    Fina y lánguida,
Como en esa noche tibia de la muerta primavera,
Como en esa noche llena de perfumes, de murmullos y de
    músicas de alas,
    Se acercó y marchó con ella,
    Se acercó y marchó con ella,
Se acercó y marchó con ella... ¡Oh las sombras enlazadas!
¡Oh las sombras que se buscan y se juntan en las noches de
    negruras y de lágrimas!...

                (De "El libro de versos")

And the dogs could be heard barking at the moon,
    At the pale moon
    And the croaking
    Of the frogs.
I felt cold, and it was the cold of your cheeks and your temples
And your adored hands in the bedroom,
    Between the snowy sheets
    Of the shroud that covered you.
    It was the cold of the tomb, it was the cold of death,
    It was the cold of nothingness…
    And my shadow ,
    Cast by the moonbeams,
    Walked alone,
    Walked alone,
    Walked alone in the solitary dunes!
    And your shadow, fine and agile,
    Slim and graceful,
Like that warm night of the now dead Spring,
Like that night full of perfumes, murmurs and music of wings,
    Came close and walked next to it,
    Came close and walked next to it,
Came close and walked next to it…Oh the two linked
    shadows!
Oh the shadows that seek each other and unite in the nights full
    of darkness and tears!..

RUBEN DARIO

AMO, AMAS

Amar, amar, amar, amar siempre, con todo
el ser y con la tierra y con el cielo,
con lo claro del sol y lo obscuro del lodo;
amar por toda ciencia y amar por todo anhelo.

Y cuando la montaña de la vida
nos sea dura y larga y alta y llena de abismos,
amar la inmensidad que es de amor encendida
¡y arder en la fusión de nuestros pechos mismos!

(De "Cantos de vida y esperanza")

RUBEN DARIO
(Nicaragua, 1867-1916)

I LOVE, YOU LOVE

To love, to love, to love, to love always, with all
your being and the earth and the sky,
with the brilliance of the sun and the darkness
of mud: to love with knowledge and to love with desire.

And when the mountain of life
is hard, long, high and full of abysses,
to love the infinity which is blazing love
and to burn in the fusion of our very own breasts!

VERSOS DE OTOÑO

Cuando mi pensamiento va hacia ti, se perfuma;
tu mirar es tan dulce, que se torna profundo.
Bajo tus pies desnudos aun hay blancor de espuma,
y en tus labios compendias la alegría del mundo.

El amor pasajero tiene el encanto breve,
y ofrece un igual término para el gozo y la pena.
Hace una hora que un nombre grabé sobre la nieve;
hace un minuto dije mi amor sobre la arena.

Las hojas amarillas caen en la alameda,
en donde vagan tantas parejas amorosas.
Y en la copa de Otoño un vago vino queda
en que han de deshojarse, Primavera, tus rosas.

(De "El canto errante")

AUTUMN VERSES

When my thought goes out to you, it is perfumed;
your gaze is so sweet, that it becomes profound.
Under your naked feet there is still a whiteness of foam,
and in your lips is gathered the joy of the world.

Passing love has a short charm,
 and offers equally delight and pain.
An hour ago I wrote a name in the snow;
a minute ago I pronounced my love on the sand.

The yellowed leaves fall on the alameda,
where so many couples stroll.
And in the cup of Autumn a vague wine remains
where the petals of your roses will be brought by the Spring.

AMADO NERVO

COBARDIA

Pasó con su madre. ¡Qué rara belleza!
¡Qué rubios cabellos de trigo garzul!
¡Qué ritmo en el paso! ¡Qué innata realeza
de porte! ¡Qué formas bajo el fino tul!...

Pasó con su madre. Volvió la cabeza:
¡me clavó muy hondo su mirada azul!

Quedé como en éxtasis...
                    Con febril premura,
"¡Síguela!", gritaron cuerpo y alma al par.
...Pero tuve miedo de amar con locura,
de abrir mis heridas, que suelen sangrar,
¡y no obstante toda mi sed de ternura,
cerrando los ojos, la dejé pasar!

(De "Serenidad")

AMADO NERVO
(Mexico, 1870-1919)

COWARDICE

She passed with her mother. What rare beauty!
What blond hair of wheat golden blond!
What rhythm in her walk! What an innate royalty
in her bearing! What a beauty under the fine tulle!

She passed with her mother. She turned her head:
her blue gaze nailed me to the very depth.

I stood in rapture...
                    With feverish rush,
"Follow her!", cried my soul and body.
But I feared falling crazily in love,
to open my wounds, which tend to bleed,
and despite all my thirst for tenderness,
I closed my eyes and I let her pass!

LEOPOLDO LUGONES

DELECTACIÓN MOROSA

La tarde con ligera pincelada
que iluminó la paz de nuestro asilo,
apuntó en su matiz crisoberilo
una sutil decoración morada.

Surgió enorme la luna en la enramada;
las hojas agravaban su sigilo,
y una araña en la punta de su hilo
tejía sobre el astro hipnotizada.

Poblóse de murciélagos el combo
cielo, a manera de chinesco biombo;
tus rodillas exangües sobre el plinto

manifestaban la delicia inerte,
y a nuestros pies un río de jacinto
corría sin rumor hacia la muerte.

(De "Los crepúsculos del jardín")

LEOPOLDO LUGONES
(Argentina, 1874-1938)

SLOW DELIGHT

The afternoon with a light brush stroke
illuminated the quiet of our sanctuary,
painting in its chrysoberyl hues
a subtle touch of violet.

The moon came out huge through the branches;
the foliage intensified its mystical light
and a spider at the end of its web
was weaving hypnotized on the celestial star.

The arched firmament was flooded with bats,
like on the surface of a Chinese folding screen;
your pale knees on the grave-stone

were a sign of the inertia of delight,
and at our feet a river of hyacinth
flowed silently toward death.

JULIO HERRERA Y REISSIG

DECORACION HERALDICA

Señora de mis pobres homenajes
débote amor aunque me ultrajes.
GONGORA

Soñé que te encontrabas junto al muro
glacial donde termina la existencia,
paseando tu magnífica opulencia
de doloroso terciopelo oscuro.

Tu pie, decoro del marfil más puro,
hería, con satánica inclemencia,
las pobres almas, llenas de paciencia,
que aún se brindaban a tu amor perjuro.

Mi dulce amor, que sigue sin sosiego,
igual que un triste corderito ciego
la huella perfumada de tu sombra,

buscó el suplicio de tu regio yugo,
y bajo el raso de tu pie verdugo
puse mi esclavo corazón de alfombra.

JULIO HERRERA Y REISSIG
(Uruguay, 1873-1910)

HERALDIC DECORATION

> *Lady of my poor dedications*
> *I owe you love even if you insult me*
> *GONGORA*

I dreamed that you were standing
by the frozen wall where life ends,
shuffling your magnificent opulence
of painful dark velvet.

Your foot, expression of the purest ivory,
scathed, with satanic cruelty,
the pure, patient souls who still
offered themselves as nourishment to your false love.

My gentle love, which follows constantly
like a sad, blind little lamb
the perfumed traces of your shadow,

sought the torment of your royal yoke,
and under the heel of your cruel foot
I spread my enslaved heart for you to step on.

AMOR SADICO

Ya no te amaba, sin dejar por eso
de amar la sombra de tu amor distante.
Ya no te amaba, y sin embargo el beso
de la repulsa nos unió un instante...

Agrio placer y bárbaro embeleso
crispó mi faz, me demudó el semblante.
Ya no te amaba, y me turbé, no obstante,
como una virgen en un bosque espeso.

Y ya perdida para siempre, al verte
anochecer en el eterno luto,
-mudo de amor, el corazón inerte-,

huraño, atroz, inexorable, hirsuto...
¡Jamás viví como en aquella muerte,
nunca te amé como en aquel minuto!

(De "Los parques abandonados")

SADISTIC LOVE

I did not love you anymore, yet I never stopped
loving the shadow of your distant love.
I did not love you anymore, yet that kiss
of denial united us for a moment...

Sour pleasure and barbarous charm
contracted my face and deadened my countenance.
I did not love you anymore, yet I was troubled
like a virgin in a dark forest.

And while you were lost forever, looking
at your walk into the night of eternal mourning
-the heart dead, love voiceless-

pitiless, heinous, rough, inexorable...
I never lived a death like that one,
and never loved you more than in that minute!

ANTONIO MACHADO

XI

Yo voy soñando caminos
de la tarde. ¡Las colinas
doradas, los verdes pinos,
las polvorientas encinas!....
¿Adónde el camino irá?

Yo voy cantando, viajero
a lo largo del sendero…
-La tarde cayendo está-.
"En el corazón tenía
"la espina de una pasión;
"logré arrancármela un día:
"ya no siento el corazón."

Y todo el campo un momento
se queda, mudo y sombrío,
meditando. Suena el viento
en los álamos del río.

La tarde más se obscurece;
y el camino que serpea
y débilmente blanquea,
se enturbia y desaparece.

Mi cantar vuelve a plañir:
"Aguda espina dorada,
"quién te pudiera sentir
"en el corazón clavada".

(De "Soledades")

ANTONIO MACHADO
(Spain, 1875-France,1939)

XI

I go on dreaming
of afternoon roads.
The golden hills and green pines,
the dusty bushes!...
Where does this road lead to?

I go on singing, a traveler
along the path
-the darkness falls-
"I had in my heart
"the thorn of a passion;
"I managed to take it out one day
"and killed my heart."

For one moment the valley stands still,
mute and sombre,
deep in thought. The wind whistles
in the poplars by the river.

It's getting darker fast;
the winding road
looks faintly white,
becomes vague and disappears.

And my song mourns:
"Sharp golden thorn,
who could have noticed you
nailed in my heart?"

EFREN REBOLLEDO

EL BESO DE SAFO

Más pulidos que el mármol transparente,
más blancos que los blancos vellocinos,
se anudan los dos cuerpos femeninos
en un grupo escultórico y ardiente.

Ancas de cebra, escorzos de serpiente,
combas rotundas, senos colombinos,
una lumbre los labios purpurinos
y las dos cabelleras un torrente.

En el vivo combate, los pezones
que se embisten, parecen dos pitones
trabados en eróticas pendencias,

y en medio de los muslos enlazados,
dos rosas de capullos inviolados
destilan y confunden sus esencias.

(De "Caro Victrix")

EFREN REBOLLEDO
(Mexico, 1877-Madrid,1929)

SAPHO'S KISS

Shinier than transparent marble,
whiter than the finest pelt,
two female bodies are intertwined
in a sculptural union of passion.

Coiled serpent, shapely thighs of zebra,
round arcs, proud pigeon breasts,
a burning fire their red lips,
and the hair of both a fervid torrent.

In this live combat, their attacking nipples
look like constricting pythons
interlinked in erotic battle.

And in their interwoven thighs,
two roses with their buds intact
distill and blend their essences.

JUAN RAMON JIMENEZ

RETORNO FUGAZ

¿Cómo era, Dios mío, cómo era?
-¡Oh, corazón falaz, mente indecisa!-
¿Era como el pasaje de la brisa?
¿Cómo la huída de la primavera?

Tan leve, tan voluble, tan ligera
cual estival vilano... ¡Sí! Imprecisa
como sonrisa que se pierde en risa...
¡Vana en el aire, igual que una bandera!

Bandera, sonreír, vilano, alada
primavera de junio, brisa pura...
¡Qué loco fue tu carnaval, qué triste!

Todo tu cambiar trocóse en nada
-¡memoria, ciega abeja de amargura!-
¡No sé cómo eras, yo que sé que fuiste!

(De "Sonetos espirituales")

JUAN RAMON JIMENEZ
(Spain, 1881-Puerto Rico, 1958)

FLEETING RETURN

How was she, my God, how was she?
-Oh, deceitful heart, uncertain mind!-
Was she like the breath of the breeze?
Like the flight of Spring?

So tiny, so voluble, so ethereal,
like a downy thorn...Yes! Vague
like a smile lost in laughter...
vain like a banner in the air!

Banner, smile, thorn, winged
Spring of June, pure breeze...
How crazy was your carnival, how sad!

All your changes came to naught
-memory, blind bee of bitterness!-
I don't know how you were, I know only that you left!

DELMIRA AGUSTINI

LA NOCHE ENTRO EN LA SALA ADORMECIDA

La noche entró en la sala adormecida
arrastrando el silencio a pasos lentos…
Los sueños son tan quedos que una herida
sangrar se oiría. Rueda en los momentos

una palabra insólita, caída
como una hoja de otoño… Pensamientos
suaves tocan mi frente dolorida,
tal manos frescas ¡ah!… ¿por qué tormentos

misteriosos los rostros palidecen
dulcemente?… tus ojos me parecen
dos semillas de luz entre la sombra,

y hay en mi alma un gran florecimiento
si en mí los fijas; si los bajas, siento
como si fuera a florecer la alfombra.

(De "Cantos de la mañana")

DELMIRA AGUSTINI
(Uruguay, 1886 - 1914)

THE NIGHT CAME IN THE DROWSY LIVING ROOM

The night came in the drowsy living room
dragging silence in a slow pace...
Dreams are so quiet that even if a wound bled
it would be heard. An unusual word

rolls in the moments; it fell
like an autumn leaf... Sweet
thoughts touch my aching brow
like a cool hand, oh!...by what dark

torments do faces become so sweetly
pale?.. Your eyes to me look like
two seeds of light in the darkness,

and if you fix these eyes on me, a blossoming
birth will enrich my soul; if you lower them,
I feel that the carpet will bloom.

EL INTRUSO

Amor, la noche estaba trágica y sollozante
cuando tu llave de oro cantó en mi cerradura;
luego, la puerta abierta sobre la sombra helante,
tu forma fue una mancha de luz y de blancura.

Todo aquí lo alumbraron tus ojos de diamante;
bebieron en mi copa tus labios de frescura,
y descansó en mi almohada tu cabeza fragante;
me encantó tu descaro y adoré tu locura.

¡Y hoy río si tú ríes, y canto si tú cantas;
y si tú duermes, duermo como un perro a tus plantas!
¡Hoy llevo hasta en mi sombra tu olor de primavera;

y tiemblo si tu mano toca la cerradura,
y bendigo la noche sollozante y oscura
que floreció en mi vida tu boca tempranera!

(De "El libro blanco")

THE INTRUDER

My love, the tragic night was crying with sobs
when your golden key sang in my lock:
then when the door opened upon the chilling shade,
your form was a spot of light and whiteness.

Everything was illuminated by your diamond eyes;
your cool lips drank from my cup,
and your fragrant head rested on my pillow;
I was enchanted by your impudence and I adored your folly.

And today I laugh when you laugh and I sing when you sing;
and if you sleep, I sleep like a dog at your feet!
Now I have even in my shadow your Spring perfume,

and I tremble if your hand touches the keyhole,
and I bless the sobbing dark night
that your eager mouth made flourish in my life.

RAMON LOPEZ VELARDE

MIENTRAS MUERE LA TARDE...

Noble señora de provincia: unidos
en el viejo balcón que ve al poniente,
hablamos tristemente, largamente,
de dichas muertas y de tiempos idos.

De los rústicos tiestos florecidos
desprendo rosas para ornar tu frente,
y hay en los fresnos del jardín de enfrente
un escándalo de aves en los nidos.

El crepúsculo cae soñoliento,
y si con tus desdenes amortiguas
la llama de mi amor, yo me contento

con el hondo mirar de tus arcanos
ojos, mientras admiro las antiguas
joyas de las abuelas en tus manos.

(De "La sangre devota")

RAMON LOPEZ VELARDE
(Mexico, 1888-1921)

IN THE DYING AFTERNOON...

Noble lady from the province: sitting together
on the old balcony that faces the sunset,
we talked at length, sadly,
of dead happiness and days gone by.

I take the roses from the laden
vases to adorn your forehead;
in the linden trees of the garden next door,
the birds squabble in their nests.

The twilight comes slowly, sleepily,
and even if you deaden with your scorn
the flame of my love, I still remain

within the deep glance of your mystical eyes,
while at the same time I admire
your grandmother's jewelry on your hands.

LA MANCHA DE PURPURA

Me impongo la costosa penitencia
de no mirarte en días y días, porque mis ojos,
cuando por fin te miren, se aneguen en tu esencia
como si naufragasen en un golfo de púrpura,
de melodía y de vehemencia.

Pasa el lunes, y el martes, y el miércoles… Yo sufro
tu eclipse ¡oh creatura solar! mas en mi duelo
el afán de mirarte se dilata
como una profecía; se descorre cual velo
paulatino; se acendra como miel; se aquilata
como la entraña de las piedras finas;
y se aguza como el llavín
de la celda de amor de un monasterio en ruinas.

Tú no sabes la dicha refinada
que hay en huirte, que hay en el furtivo gozo
de adorarte furtivamente, de cortejarte
más allá de la sombra, de bajarse el embozo
una vez por semana, y exponer las pupilas,
en un minuto fraudulento,
a la mancha de púrpura de tu deslumbramiento.

En el bosque de amor, soy cazador furtivo;
te acecho entre dormidos y tupidos follajes,
como se acecha un ave fúlgida; y de estos viajes
por la espesura, traigo a mi aislamiento
el más fúlgido de los plumajes:
el plumaje de púrpura de tu deslumbramiento.

THE PURPLE SPOT

I impose on myself the costly punishment
not to look at you for days and days, so that my eyes,
when they finally see you, may drown in your essence
as if they were shipwrecked in a purple gulf
of melody and passion.

Monday is gone and Tuesday, and Wednesday...I suffer
your eclipse, oh solar existence! but in my grief
the desire yearning to look at you is magnified
like a prophecy; it is drawn like a slow veil; it's purified
like honey; it's valued like the innards of precious stones;
and it's severed like the lock in love's cell
of a ruined monastery.

You don't know the chosen luck
that exists in the flight from you, that exists in the pleasure
to adore you secretly, to flirt with you
beyond the shadow, to lower the hood
once a week and expose only the pupils of my eyes,
for a fleeting moment,
in the incandescent spot of your glow.

I am a clandestine hunter in the forest of love;
I watch you waiting in ambush within thick, sleeping bushes
as one watches a resplendent bird; and from these trips
through the foliage, I bring back to my isolation
the most resplendent plumage:
the purple plumage of your brightness.

MI CORAZON SE AMERITA...

A Rafael López

Mi corazón, leal, se amerita en la sombra.
Yo lo sacara al día, como lengua de fuego
que se saca de un ínfimo purgatorio a la luz;
y al oírlo batir su cárcel, yo me anego
y me hundo en la ternura remordida de un padre
que siente, entre sus brazos, latir un hijo ciego.

Mi corazón, leal, se amerita en la sombra.
Placer, amor, dolor... todo le es ultraje
y estimula su cruel carrera logarítmica,
sus ávidas mareas y su eterno oleaje.

Mi corazón, leal, se amerita en la sombra.
Es la mitra y la válvula... yo me lo arrancaría
para llevarlo en triunfo a conocer el día,
la estola de violetas en los hombros del alba,
el cíngulo morado de los atardeceres,
los astros, y el perímetro jovial de las mujeres.

Mi corazón, leal, se amerita en la sombra.
Desde una cumbre enhiesta yo lo he de lanzar
como sangriento disco a la hoguera solar.
Así extirparé el cáncer de mi fatiga dura,
seré impasible por el Este y el Oeste,
asistiré con una sonrisa depravada
a las ineptitudes de la inepta cultura,
y habrá en mi corazón la llama que le preste
el incendio sinfónico de la esfera celeste.

(De "Zozobra")

MY HEART, FAITHFUL...

A Rafael López

My heart, faithful, has earned itself the shadow
I would have exposed it to the daylight like a tongue of fire
that emerges from an infamous purgatory to light;
and listening to it knock at its prison, I choke
and sink in the repentant tenderness of a father
holding a blind child in his arms.

My heart, faithful, has earned itself the shadow.
Delight, love, pain...extremes to my heart
that stimulates its cruel, logarithmic running,
its avid tides and its eternal waves.

My heart, faithful, has earned itself the shadow.
It is the mitre and the valve...I would uproot it
triumphantly to let it recognize the day,
the shawl of violets on dawn's shoulders,
the violet waist of sunsets,
the stars and the joyful perimeter of women.

My heart, faithful, has earned itself the shadow.
From a tall mountain top I will hurl it
like a bloody disc to the flames of the sun.
Thus I will uproot the cancer of my cruel tiredness,
I will become indifferent to sunrise or sunset,
I will help with an evil smile
the improprieties of the valueless civilization,
and my heart will burn the flame
it borrowed from the symphonic fire of the celestial globe.

ENRIQUE BANCHS

BALBUCEO

Triste está la casa nuestra,
triste, desde que te has ido.
Todavía queda un poco
de tu calor en el nido.

Yo también estoy un poco
triste desde que te has ido;
pero sé que alguna tarde
llegarás de nuevo al nido.

¡Si supieras cuánto, cuánto
la casa y yo te queremos!
Algún día cuando vuelvas
verás cuánto te queremos.

Nunca podría decirte
todo lo que te queremos:
es como un montón de estrellas
todo lo que te queremos.

Si tú no volvieras nunca,
más vale que yo me muera…;
pero siento que no quieres,
no quieres que yo me muera.

Bienquerida que te fuiste,
¿no es cierto que volverás?;
para que no estemos tristes
¿no es cierto que volverás?

(De "El cascabel del halcón")

ENRIQUE BANCHS
(Argentina,1888-1968)

MUMBLING

Sad is our home,
sad, since you left.
Still, a little of your warmth
remains in our nest.

I, too, am a bit sad
since you left, but I know
that one evening
you'll return to our nest.

If you only knew how much,
the house and I love you!
When you return some day,
you'll find out, as I told you.

I could never tell you how much
the house and I love you:
like a mount of stars
is our love for you.

But if you never come back, never,
I would rather die;...
yet, I feel that you don't wish
no, you don't want me to die.

Dear beloved who is now gone,
you will return, won't you?
So our lives will not be of grief,
isn't it true that you will return?

GABRIELA MISTRAL

AMO AMOR

Anda libre en el surco, bate el ala en el viento,
late vivo en el sol y se prende al pinar.
No te vale olvidarlo como al mal pensamiento:
¡le tendrás que escuchar!

Habla lengua de bronce y habla lengua de ave,
ruegos tímidos, imperativos de mar.
No te vale ponerle gesto audaz, ceño grave:
¡lo tendrás que hospedar!

Gasta trazas de dueño; no le ablandan excusas.
Rasga vasos de flor, hiende el hondo glaciar.
No te vale decirle que albergarlo rehúsas:
¡lo tendrás que hospedar!

Tiene argucias sutiles en la réplica fina,
argumentos de sabio, pero en voz de mujer.
Ciencia humana te salva, menos ciencia divina:
¡le tendrás que creer!

Te echa venda de lino; tú la venda toleras.
Te ofrece el brazo cálido, no le sabes huir.
Echa a andar, tú le sigues hechizada aunque vieras
¡que eso para en morir!

GABRIELA MISTRAL
(Chile, 1889 -Hempstead, New York, 1957)

I LOVE, LOVE

He runs free in the furrow, flutters his wings in the air,
he pulsates in the sun and gets caught in the pine grove.
It does not help to forget him like a bad thought:
you must listen to him!

He speaks a language of bronze and a language of birds,
timid entreaties, commands of the sea.
It doesn't help to get mad or frown at him:
you must give him lodging!

His disposition is that of a master; words do not soften him.
He rips flower-pots and gashes deep glaciers.
It doesn't help to tell him that you have no bed for him :
you must give him lodgings.

He has subtle sophistries in his sharp retorts,
wise arguments, but in a woman's voice.
Human science, not the divine one can save you:
you must believe him!

He places a linen blindfold on you, and you accept it.
He offers you his arm, you cannot escape him.
He leaves. Entranced you follow him though you see
that this will end in death!

BALADA

El pasó con otra;
yo le vi pasar.
Siempre dulce el viento
y el camino en paz.
¡Y estos ojos míseros
le vieron pasar!

El va amando a otra
por la tierra en flor.
Ha abierto el espino;
pasa una canción.
¡Y él va amando a otra
por la tierra en flor!

El besó a la otra
a orillas del mar,
resbaló en las olas
la luna de azahar.
¡Y no untó mi sangre
la extensión del mar!

El irá con otra
por la eternidad.
Habrá cielos dulces.
(Dios quiere callar.)
¡Y él irá con otra
por la eternidad!

(De "Desolación")

BALLAD

He was strolling with another woman;
I saw him go by.
The wind gentle as always
the road peaceful.
And these miserable eyes
saw him go by!

Yes, he loves another
in this flowering earth,
the hawthorn is in bloom,
a tune is heard.
And he loves another
in this flowering earth!

He kissed the other one
at the seashore;
the lemon blossomed moon
glides on the waves.
My blood is not anointed
by the boundless sea.

He will go to eternity
with another one.
Heavens will be sweet
(God will be silent.)
And he will go to eternity
with another one!

ALFONSINA STORNI

LA CARICIA PERDIDA

Se me va de los dedos la caricia sin causa,
se me va de los dedos… En el viento, al rodar,
la caricia que vaga sin destino ni objeto,
la caricia perdida, ¿quién la recogerá?

Pude amar esta noche con piedad infinita,
pude amar al primero que acertara a llegar.
Nadie llega. Están solos los floridos senderos.
La caricia perdida, rodará…, rodará…

Si en el viento te llaman esta noche, viajero,
si estremece las ramas un dulce suspirar,
si te oprime los dedos una mano pequeña
que te toma y te deja, que te logra y se va.

Si no ves esa mano, ni la boca que besa,
si es el aire quien teje la ilusión de llamar,
oh, viajero, que tienes como el cielo los ojos,
en el viento fundida, ¿me reconocerás?

(De "Languidez")

ALFONSINA STORNI
(Argentina, 1892-1938)

THE LOST CARESS

The aimless caress slips through my fingers,
it slips through my fingers as it rolls into the wind,
the caress wanders with no aim, nor any future,
who shall find and take the lost caress?

I could love tonight with infinite compassion,
I could love the first one I meet.
But no one comes. There is loneliness in the flowering paths.
The lost caress, will roll...and roll...

If in the wind they call you tonight, traveler,
if a gentle sigh quivers in the boughs,
if a small hand grips your fingers
holding you, letting go, finding, losing you.

If you don't see that hand, nor the kissing lips,
if the calling is naught but an illusion of the wind,
oh, traveler with the blue eyes,
scattered in the wind, will you recognize me?

CESAR VALLEJO

IDILIO MUERTO

Qué estará haciendo esta hora mi andina y dulce Rita
de junco y capulí;
ahora que me asfixia Bizancio, y que dormita
la sangre, como flojo cognac, dentro de mí.

Dónde estarán sus manos que en actitud contrita
planchaban en las tardes blancuras por venir;
ahora, en esta lluvia que me quita
las ganas de vivir.

Qué será de su falda de franela; de sus
afanes; de su andar;
de su sabor a cañas de Mayo del lugar.

Ha de estarse a la puerta mirando algún celaje,
y al fin dirá temblando "¡Qué frío hay... Jesús!"
Y llorará en las tejas un pájaro salvaje.

(De "Los heraldos negros")

CESAR VALLEJO
(Peru, 1892 - París, 1938)

DEAD IDYLL

What could my sweet Andean Rita of rush and blackberries
 be doing now? Now that Byzantium
chokes me and the blood, like a flat cognac
is sleeping in my veins.

Where could her hands be, which in an attitude of penitence
would iron in the evening whitenesses to come;
now, in this rain which drives away
my will to live.

What became of her flannel robe;
of her toils; of her stride; of her taste of sugarcanes in May.

She must be at the door looking at some omen,
and shivering in the end will say: "Jesús...how cold!"
and a wild bird will cry on the roof.

XV

En el rincón aquel, donde dormimos juntos
tantas noches, ahora me he sentado
a caminar. La cuja de los novios difuntos
fue sacada, o tal vez qué habrá pasado.

Has venido temprano a otros asuntos
y ya no estás. Es el rincón
donde a tu lado, leí una noche,
entre tus tiernos puntos,
un cuento de Daudet. Es el rincón
amado. No lo equivoques.

Me he puesto a recordar los días
de verano idos, tu entrar y salir,
poca y harta pálida por los cuartos.

En esta noche pluviosa,
ya lejos de ambos dos, salto de pronto…
Son dos puertas abriéndose cerrándose,
dos puertas que al viento van y vienen
sombra   a   sombra.

(De "Trilce")

XV

In that corner where we slept together
many a night, I sit down now
to walk. The bed of the dead lovers
was taken away, or whatever happened to it.

You came early, for other matters
and you are no more. It is the corner
where one night, by your side, I read
between your tender nipples
a short story of Daudet. It is the beloved
corner. Do not mistake it.

I set myself to recall the summer
days that are gone, your comings and goings,
small and big and pale in the rooms.

In this rainy night,
away from us both, I jump up from my sleep…
There are two doors that open and close,
two doors that come and go in the wind
darkness   to   darkness.

VICENTE HUIDOBRO

ALTAZOR, *CANTO II* (Fragmentos)

Mujer el mundo está amueblado por tus ojos
Se hace más alto el cielo en tu presencia
La tierra se prolonga de rosa en rosa
Y el aire se prolonga de paloma de paloma

Al irte dejas una estrella en tu sitio
Dejas caer tus luces como el barco que pasa
Mientras te sigue mi canto embrujado
Como una serpiente fiel y melancólica
Y tú vuelves la cabeza detrás de algún astro

¿Qué combate se libra en el espacio?
Esas lanzas de luz entre planetas
Reflejo de armaduras despiadadas
¡Qué estrella sanguinaria no quiere ceder el paso?
En dónde estás triste noctámbula
Dadora de infinito
Que pasea en el bosque de los sueños

Heme aquí perdido entre mares desiertos
Solo como la pluma que se cae de un pájaro en la noche
Heme aquí en una torre de frío
Abrigado del recuerdo de tus labios marítimos
Del recuerdo de tus complacencias y de tu cabellera
Luminosa y desatada como los ríos de montaña
¿Irías a ser ciega que Dios te dio esas manos?
Te pregunto otra vez
El arco de tus cejas tendido para las armas de los ojos
En la ofensiva alada vencedora segura con orgullos de flor
Te hablan por mí las piedras aporreadas
Te hablan por mí las olas de pájaros sin cielo
Te habla por mí el color de los paisajes sin viento
Te habla por mí el rebaño de ovejas taciturnas

VICENTE HUIDOBRO
(Chile, 1893-1948)

ALTAZOR, *CANTO II*   (excerpts)

Woman the world is furnished by your eyes
The sky becomes loftier in your presence
The earth expands from rose to rose
And the air is prolonged from dove to dove

When you go away you leave a star in your place
You throw your lights like a passing ship
While my song follows you enchanted
Like a faithful and melancholic serpent
And you turn your head to see behind some star

What titanic battle is unleashed in space?
Those blades of light between planets
Reflections from merciless armors
Which bloody star bars your passage?
Where are you roaming sad sleepwalker
Giver of infinity
Wandering in the forest of dreams

Here I am lost in deserted seas
Alone as a feather falling from a bird at night
Here I am on a freezing tower
Dressed in the memory of your briny lips
In the memory of your hair and your care
Glowing and gushing from the mountain like the rivers
Were you to be born blind that God gave you these hands?
I ask you again
Your eyebrows' arch stretched for the arrows of your eyes
In the winged attack certain victorious and with the pride of a
        flower
Scalped stones speak to you of me
The waves of skyless birds speak to you for me
The color of the windless landscapes speak to you of me
And the herd of speechless sheep speak to you of me

Tengo una atmósfera propia de tu aliento
La fabulosa seguridad de tu mirada con sus constelaciones
    íntimas
Con su propio lenguaje de semilla
Tu frente luminosa como un anillo de Dios
Más firme que todo en la flora del cielo
Sin torbellinos de universo que se encabrita
Como un caballo a causa de su sombra en el aire

Te pregunto otra vez
¿Irías a ser muda que Dios te dio esos ojos?

Tengo esa voz tuya para toda defensa
Esa voz que sale de ti en latidos de corazón
Esa voz en que cae la eternidad
Y se rompe en pedazos de esferas fosforescentes
¿Qué sería la vida si no hubieras nacido?
Un cometa sin manto muriéndose de frío
Te hallé como una lágrima en un libro olvidado
Con tu nombre sensible desde antes en mi pecho
Tu nombre hecho del ruido de palomas que se vuelan
Traes en ti el recuerdo de otras vidas más altas
De un Dios encontrado en alguna parte
Y al fondo de ti misma recuerdas que eras tú
El pájaro de antaño en la clave del poeta

Sueño en un sueño sumergido
La cabellera que se ata hace el día
La cabellera al desatarse hace la noche
La vida se contempla en el olvido
Sólo viven tus ojos en el mundo
El único sistema planetario sin fatiga
Serena piel anclada en las alturas
Ajena a toda red y estratagema
En su fuerza de luz ensimismada
Detrás de ti la vida siente miedo
Porque eres la profundidad de toda cosa

My atmosphere is that of your breath
The mythical certainty of your glance with its own intimate
    constellations
With its own language of seed
Your luminous brow like a God's ring
Firmer than all heavenly flora
Without the universal whirlwinds rearing
Like a horse startled by your shadow.

I ask you again
Were you ordained to be mute that God gave you these eyes?
I have your voice for my defense
The voice which comes from you in the beats of the heart
That voice where eternity falls
And shatters into phosphorescent stars

How would life be if you were not born?
A comet without a mantle dying of cold
I find you like a tear in a forgotten book
Already feeling your name in my breast
Your name created from the sound of pigeons in flight
Deep in your inner self you carry the memory of other loftier
    lives
Of a God who exists somewhere
And deep within you lives the remembrance that you were
The bird of yore in the poet's code

I dream deep within another dream
The hair which binds the depth of day
The hair which releases the depth of night
Life is contemplated in oblivion
Only your eyes live in the world
The only planetary system without weariness
Serene skin anchored in infinity
Alien to every net and stratagem
In its strength of vain light
Behind you life is frightened
Because you are the depth of everything

El mundo deviene majestuoso cuando pasas
Se oyen caer lágrimas del cielo
Y borras en el alma adormecida
La amargura de ser vivo
Se hace liviano el orbe en las espaldas
....

Mi gloria está en tus ojos
Vestida del lujo de tus ojos y de su brillo interno
Estoy sentado en el rincón más sensible de tu mirada
Bajo el silencio estático de inmóviles pestañas
Viene saliendo un augurio del fondo de tus ojos
Y un viento de océano ondula tus pupilas

Nada se compara a esa leyenda de semillas que deja tu
          presencia
A esa voz que busca un astro muerto que volver a la vida
Tu voz hace un imperio en el espacio
Y esa mano que se levanta en ti como si fuera a colgar soles en
          el aire
Y ese mirar que escribe mundos en el infinito
Y esa cabeza que se dobla para escuchar un murmullo en la
          eternidad
Y ese pie que es la fiesta de los caminos encadenados
Y esos párpados donde vienen a vararse las centellas del éter
Y ese beso que hincha la proa de sus labios
Y esa sonrisa como un estandarte al frente de tu vida
Y ese secreto que dirige las mareas de tu pecho
Dormido a la sombra de tus senos

Si tú murieras
Las estrellas a pesar de su lámpara encendida
Perderían el camino
¿Qué sería del universo?

                              (De "Altazor")

The world gains in majesty when you pass
Tears are heard as they fall from heaven
And in your sleeping soul you extinguish
The bitterness of life
Infinity becomes lighter on the shoulders

....

My glory is in your eyes
Dressed with the luxury of your eyes and their inner glow
I'm riveted in the most penetrating sector of your glance
Under the static silence of motionless eyebrows
A prophesy is rising from the depth of your eyes
An oceanic wind waves their pupils

Nothing compares with the legend of seeds left by your
        presence
With that voice which tries to give life to a dead star
Your voice creates an empire in the void
And that hand lifted by you as if to hang suns in the air
And that glance drawing worlds in infinity
And that head bending to hear a whisper in eternity
And that foot that is the feast of the interlinked streets
And those eyelashes where the air sparks are entrenched
And that kiss which swells the prow of your lips
And that smile that flutters like a flag between your life
And that secret that directs the tidal swelling of your chest
Sleeping in the shade of your breasts.

If you were to die
The stars despite their brightness
Would lose their way
What then would become of the universe?

GERARDO DIEGO

INSOMNIO

Tú y tu desnudo sueño. No lo sabes.
Duermes. No. No lo sabes. Yo en desvelo,
y tú, inocente, duermes bajo el cielo.
Tú por tu sueño y por el mar las naves.

En cárceles de espacio, aéreas llaves
te me encierran, recluyen, roban. Hielo,
cristal de aire en mil hojas. No. No hay vuelo
que alce hasta ti las alas de mis aves.

Saber que duermes tú, cierta, segura
-cauce fiel de abandono, línea pura-,
tan cerca de mis brazos maniatados.

Qué pavorosa esclavitud de isleño,
yo insomne, loco, en los acantilados,
las naves por el mar, tú por tu sueño.

(De "Alondra de verdad")

GERARDO DIEGO
(Spain, 1896-1987)

SLEEPLESSNESS

You and your naked sleep. You don't know it.
You sleep. No. You don't know it. I am awake,
and you, innocent, sleep under the heavenly dome.
You in your sleep and the ships in their sea.

Keys of wind keep you locked in prisons of void,
they keep you away from me, they steal you.
Ice, crystals of air in thousands of leaves. No. There isn't
a flight to lift up to you the wings of my birds.

To know that you sleep, certain, secure
-faithful riverbed abandonment, pure line-
so close to my chained hands.

What a horrible slavery of an islander,
I awake, crazed, in the precipitous rocks,
the ships in their sea, you in your sleep.

LUIS PALES MATOS

EL LLAMADO

Me llaman desde allá…
larga voz de hoja seca,
mano fugaz de nube
que en el aire de otoño se dispersa.
Por arriba el llamado
tira de mí con tenue hilo de estrella,
abajo, el agua en tránsito,
con sollozo de espuma entre la niebla.
Ha tiempo oigo las voces
y descubro las señas.

Hoy recuerdo: es un día venturoso
de cielo despejado y clara tierra;
golondrinas erráticas
el calmo azul puntean.
Estoy frente a la mar y en lontananza
se va perdiendo el ala de una vela;
va yéndose, esfumándose,
y yo también me voy borrando en ella.
Y cuando al fin retorno
por un leve resquicio de conciencia
¡cuán lejos ya me encuentro de mí mismo!
¡qué mundo tan extraño me rodea!

LUIS PALES MATOS
(Puerto Rico, 1898-1959)

THE CALLING

They call me from there...
far away voice of a dry leaf,
a cloud's furtive hand
dispersed in the Autumn air.
The voice from above
pulls me like a gentle thread of a star,
below, the passing water,
with the sob of foam in the mist.
For a long time now I hear the voices
and discover the signs.

Today I remember: it is a happy day
of splendid skies and luminous earth;
wandering swallows
punctuate the serene blue.
I am facing the sea and far away
the wing of a sail disappears;
it is traveling, it leaves, evaporates,
but I, too, I'm erased inside it.
And when I finally return
from a small crack of conscience
how far away I am from myself!
What a strange world surrounds me!

Ahora, dormida junto a mí, reposa
mi amor sobre la hierba.
El seno palpitante
sube y baja tranquilo en la marea
del ímpetu calmado que diluye
espectrales añiles en su ojera.
Miro esa dulce fábrica rendida,
cuerpo de trampa y presa
cuyo ritmo esencial como jugando
manufactura la caricia aérea,
el arrullo narcótico y el beso
-víspera ardiente de gozosa queja-
y me digo: Ya todo ha terminado…
Mas de pronto, despierta,
y allá en el negro hondón de sus pupilas
que son un despedirse y una ausencia,
algo me invita a su remota margen
y dulcemente, sin querer, me lleva.

Me llaman desde allá…
Mi nave aparejada está dispuesta.
A su redor, en grumos de silencio,
sordamente coagula la tiniebla.
Un mar hueco, sin peces,
agua vacía y negra
sin vena de fulgor que la penetre
ni pisada de brisa que la mueva.
Fondo inmóvil de sombra,
límite gris de piedra…
¡Oh soledad, que a fuerza de andar sola
se siente de sí misma compañera!

Now, sleeping next to me,
my love rests on the grass.
The pulsating chest goes up and down tranquil
in the tide of the peaceful impetus that dilutes
spectral indigoes in the circle of her eyes.
I look at this subdued factory of sweetness,
body of trap and plunder
whose basic rhythm playfully constructs
the ethereal caress,
the hypnotic rocking and the kiss
-ardent prelude of a cry of delight-
and I say to myself: all is finished...
But suddenly, she awakes,
and in the black center of her eyes,
that are a goodbye and an absence,
something calls me to their distant shore
and gently takes me, unwillingly, something takes me.

They call me from there...
My rigged boat is ready.
Around it in clots of silence,
darkness, mute, thickens.
A sea void of fish,
a sea of black water,
without a vein of light to penetrate it
not even a squashed breeze to stir it.
A still bottom of shadow,
gray border of stone...
Oh, solitude going alone out of spite
so much that she feels a companion to herself.

Emisario solícito que vienes
con oculto mensaje hasta mi puerta,
sé lo que te propones
y no me engaña tu misión secreta;
me llaman desde allá,
pero el amor dormido aquí en la hierba
es bello todavía
y un júbilo de sol baña la tierra.
¡Déjeme tu implacable poderío
una hora, un minuto más con ella!

(De "Poesía")

Diligent emissary coming to my door
with a secret message,
I know what you'll propose
and your secret mission does not deceive me;
they call me from there,
but my love sleeping on the grass
is still beautiful
and a sundrenched joy fills the earth.
Leave your merciless power
one hour, one minute more with her!

FEDERICO GARCIA LORCA

BALADILLA DE LOS TRES RIOS

El río Guadalquivir
va entre naranjos y olivos
Los dos ríos de Granada
bajan de la nieve al trigo.

¡Ay, amor
que se fue y no vino!

El río Guadalquivir
tiene las barbas granates.
Los dos ríos de Granada,
uno llanto y otro sangre.

¡Ay, amor
que se fue por el aire!

Para los barcos de vela,
Sevilla tiene un camino;
por el agua de Granada
sólo reman los suspiros.

¡Ay, amor
que se fue y no vino!

Guadalquivir, alta torre
y viento en los naranjales.
Dauro y Genil, torrecillas
muertas sobre los estanques.

¡Ay, amor
que se fue por el aire!

¡Quién dirá que el agua lleva
un fuego fatuo de gritos!

FEDERICO GARCÍA LORCA
(Spain, 1898-1936)

LITTLE BALLAD OF THE THREE RIVERS

The river Guadalquivir
flows among orangetrees and olivegroves.
The two rivers of Granada
descend from the snows to wheat fields.

Oh, love
that goes and goes and never returns!

The river Guadalquivir
has a garnet-colored beard.
The two rivers of Granada,
one is tears, the other blood.

Oh, love
that has gone with the wind!

For the sail boats
Seville has a road;
on the waters of Granada
only sighs are rowing.

Oh, love
that goes and goes and never returns!

Guadalquivir is a lofty tower;
it is the wind of the orange groves.
Dauro and Genil are little towers
dead in the ponds.

Oh, love
that has gone with the wind!

Who will say that the water
bears fire of laments!

¡Ay, amor
que se fue y no vino!

Lleva azahar, lleva olivas,
Andalucía, a tus mares.

¡Ay, amor
que se fue por el aire!

(De "Poema del Cante jondo")

SONETO DE LA DULCE QUEJA

Tengo miedo a perder la maravilla
de tus ojos de estatua, y el acento
que de noche me pone en la mejilla
la solitaria rosa de tu aliento.

Tengo pena de ser en esta orilla
tronco sin ramas; y lo que más siento
es no tener la flor, pulpa o arcilla,
para el gusano de mi sufrimiento.

Si tú eres el tesoro oculto mío,
si eres mi cruz y mi dolor mojado,
si soy el perro de tu señorío,

no me dejes perder lo que he ganado
y decora las aguas de tu río
con hojas de mi otoño enajenado.

Oh, love
that goes and goes and never returns!

It carries the olives and the lemon blossoms,
Andalucia, to your seas.

Oh, love
that has gone with the wind!

SONNET OF SWEET COMPLAINT

I am afraid to lose the marvel
of your eyes of statue or the tone
that at night poses on my cheek
the lonely rose of your breath.

It saddens me to be on this bank,
a trunk without boughs and suffer
for not having juices, clay or flowers
for this grief-moth that eats up my heart.

If you are my hidden treasure,
if you are my crucifixion and my living pain,
if I am just the dog of your domain,

don't let me lose what I gained
and adorn the stream of your river
with the dead leaves of my autumn.

ELEGIA A DOÑA JUANA LA LOCA

Diciembre de 1918
(Granada)

A Melchor Fernández Almagro

Princesa enamorada sin ser correspondida.
Clavel rojo en un valle profundo y desolado.
La tumba que te guarda rezuma tu tristeza
a través de los ojos que ha abierto sobre el mármol.

Eras una paloma con alma gigantesca
cuyo nido fue sangre del suelo castellano,
derramaste tu fuego sobre un cáliz de nieve
y al querer alentarlo tus alas se troncharon.

Soñabas que tu amor fuera como el infante
que te sigue sumiso recogiendo tu manto.
Y en vez de flores, versos y collares de perlas,
te dio la Muerte rosas marchitas en un ramo.

Tenías en el pecho la formidable aurora
de Isabel de Segura. Melibea. Tu canto,
como alondra que mira quebrarse el horizonte,
se torna de repente monótono y amargo.

Y tu grito estremece los cimientos de Burgos.
Y oprime la salmodia del coro cartujano.
Y choca con los ecos de las lentas campanas
perdiéndose en la sombra tembloroso y rasgado.

Tenías la pasión que da el cielo de España.
La pasión del puñal, de la ojera y el llanto.
¡Oh princesa divina de crepúsculo rojo,
con la rueca de hierro y de acero lo hilado!

ELEGY FOR JOAN THE MAD ONE

To Melchor Fernandez Almagro

Princess that your love was not responded.
Red carnation of a deep, desolate valley.
The tomb holding you distills your sorrow
through the eyes opened on the corroded marble.

You were a dove with a giant soul
that had for a nest the blood and soil of Castille.
You scattered your fire on a bud of snow.
When you wanted to revive it you lost your wings.

You dreamed of the love of an obedient knight
who would follow you holding the tail of your mantle.
And instead of flowers, verses and pearls,
death gave you a bouquet of withered roses.

You were holding in your heart the terrible dawn
of Isabelle de Segura. And your song, oh Melibea,
like the lark watching the horizon breaking up,
all of a sudden becomes sad and bitter.

Your scream makes the whole of Burgos shiver to its
        foundations,
it fills with sorrow the song of a monastery chorus,
and collides with the slow sound of the bells
and shattered, trembling, it fades away in the shade.

You had the passion of the sky of Spain.
The passion of the dagger, of black-circled eyes and crying.
Oh, divine princess of red twilight,
with your iron distaff and steel thread.

Nunca tuviste el nido, ni el madrigal doliente,
ni el laúd juglaresco que solloza lejano.
Tu juglar fue un mancebo con escamas de plata
y un eco de trompeta su acento enamorado.

Y, sin embargo, estabas para el amor formada,
hecha para el suspiro, el mimo y el desmayo,
para llorar tristeza sobre el pecho querido
deshojando una rosa de olor entre los labios.

Para mirar la luna bordada sobre el río
y sentir la nostalgia que en sí lleva el rebaño
y mirar los eternos jardines de la sombra,
¡oh princesa morena que duermes bajo el mármol!

¿Tienes los ojos negros abiertos a la luz?
O se enredan serpientes a tus senos exhaustos…
¿Dónde fueron tus besos lanzados a los vientos?
¿Dónde fue la tristeza de tu amor desgraciado?
En el cofre de plomo, dentro de tu esqueleto,
tendrás el corazón partido en mil pedazos.

Y Granada te guarda como santa reliquia,
¡oh princesa morena que duermes bajo el mármol!
Eloísa y Julieta fueron dos margaritas,
pero tú fuiste un rojo clavel ensangrentado
que vino de la tierra dorada de Castilla
a dormir entre nieve y ciprerales castos.

Granada era tu lecho de muerte, Doña Juana,
los cipreses, tus cirios;
la sierra, tu retablo.
Un retablo de nieve que mitigue tus ansias,
¡con el agua que pasa junto a ti! ¡La del Dauro!

Granada era tu lecho de muerte, Doña Juana,
la de las torres viejas y del jardín callado,
la de la yedra muerta sobre los muros rojos,
la de la niebla azul y el arrayán romántico.

You never had a nest, a sad song, nor the lute
 of a troubadour mourning in the distance.
Your troubadour was a youth with silver chest
and the sound of a trumpet his only words of love.

Still you were born for love,
for the sigh, the caress and the fainting,
for crying on a beloved chest, stripping off
the petals of a fragrant rose with your lips.

You were born to watch the moon embroidered on the river,
to feel the nostalgia of the leaving packs,
to watch the eternal gardens of shade,
oh, brunette princess sleeping in the tomb!

Do you have your black eyes open to the light?
Do snakes entangle on your chest?
Where are the kisses you were sending to the wind?
Where is the sorrow of your failed love?
In your leaden casket, in your skeleton,
your heart slowly melted away.

Granada holds you like a sacred relic,
oh, brunette princess sleeping in the tomb!
Eloise and Juliet were two daisies,
but you were a blood- red carnation
that came from the golden land of Castille
to sleep under the snow, among the cypress groves,

Granada was your funereal bed, oh Joan,
the cypress trees your candles, the mountains your altar.
A snow covered altar to calm your agonies
with the water of Dauro passing at your side!

Granada was your funereal bed, oh Joan,
with its old castles and sleeping gardens,
with the dead ivy on the brick walls,
with its blue mist and the romantic myrtles.

Princesa enamorada y mal correspondida.
Clavel rojo en un valle profundo y desolado.
La tumba que te guarda rezuma tu tristeza
a través de los ojos que ha abierto sobre el mármol.

(De "Libro de poemas")

LUIS CERNUDA

SI EL HOMBRE PUDIERA DECIR

Si el hombre pudiera decir lo que ama,
Si el hombre pudiera levantar su amor por el cielo
Como una nube en la luz;
Si como muros que se derrumban,
Para saludar la verdad erguida en medio,
Pudiera derrumbar su cuerpo, dejando sólo la verdad de su
        amor,
La verdad de sí mismo,
Que no se llama gloria, fortuna o ambición,
Sino amor o deseo,
Yo sería aquel que imaginaba;
Aquel que con su lengua, sus ojos y sus manos
Proclama ante los hombres la verdad ignorada,
La verdad de su amor verdadero.

Libertad no conozco sino la libertad de estar preso en alguien
Cuyo nombre no puedo oír sin escalofrío;
Alguien por quien me olvido de esta existencia mezquina,
Por quien el día y la noche son para mí lo que quiera,
Y mi cuerpo y espíritu flotan en su cuerpo y espíritu
Como leños perdidos que el mar anega o levanta
Libremente, con la libertad del amor,
La única libertad que me exalta,
La única libertad porque muero.
Tú justificas mi existencia:
Si no te conozco, no he vivido;
Si muero sin conocerte, no muero porque no he vivido.

Princess that your love was not responded.
Red carnation of a deep desolate valley.
The tomb holding you distills your sorrow
through the eyes opened on the corroded marble.

LUIS CERNUDA
(Spain, 1902 - Mexico City, 1963)

IF MAN COULD NAME

If man could name what he loves,
If man could raise his love to the sky
Like a cloud in the light;
If like walls crumbling in ruins,
To salute the truth as it stands in the middle,
He could tear his own body, leaving only the truth of his love,
The truth of himself,
Which is not called fame, ambition or luck,
But love or desire,
I would be the one he had imagined;
He who with his tongue, his eyes and his hands
Proclaims to the world the unknown truth,
The truth of his true love.

I know no other freedom than that of one being imprisoned by
        someone
Whose name I cannot hear without shivering.
Someone who makes me forget this miserable existence,
For whom day and night are for me what he wants them to be,
And my spirit and body float in his spirit and body
Like lost logs which the sea sinks or makes float
Freely, with the freedom of love,
The only freedom that exalts me,
The only freedom because I die.
You justify my existence:
If I don't get to know you, I have not lived;
If I die without knowing you, I do not die because I have not
        lived.

JORGE CARRERA ANDRADE

CUERPO DE LA AMANTE
(Fragmentos)

IV

Tu cuerpo eternamente está bañándose
en la cascada de tu cabellera,
agua lustral que baja
acariciando peñas.
La cascada quisiera ser un águila
pero sus finas alas desfallecen:
agonía de seda
sobre el desierto ardiente de tu espalda.

La cascada quisiera ser un árbol,
toda una selva en llamas
con sus lenguas lamiendo
tu armadura de plata
de joven combatiente victoriosa,
única soberana de la tierra.
Tu cuerpo se consume eternamente
entre las llamas de tu cabellera.

VI

Tu cuerpo es templo de oro,
catedral del amor
en donde entro de hinojos.

Esplendor entrevisto
de la verdad sin velos:
¡Qué profusión de lirios!

JORGE CARRERA ANDRADE
(Ecuador, 1902-1978)

THE BODY OF THE BELOVED
(Excerpts)

IV

Your body is bathed eternally
in the cascade of your hair,
lustral water that descends
caressing rocks.
The cascade wants to be an eagle
but its fine wings die,
a silken agony
on the incandescent desert of your back.

The cascade wants to be a tree,
a whole forest in flames
with its tongues of fire licking
your silver panoply
of young victorious amazon,
unique queen of the earth.
Your body is eternally consumed
by the flames of your hair.

VI

Your body is a golden temple,
a cathedral of love
where I enter on my knees.

It is a half seen splendor
of truth without veils.
What a profusion of lilies!

¡Cuántas secretas lámparas
bajo tu piel, esferas
pintadas por el alba!

Viviente, único templo:
La deidad y el devoto
suben juntos al cielo.

VII

Tu cuerpo es un jardín, masa de flores
y juncos animados.
Dominio del amor: en sus collados
persigo los eternos resplandores.

Agua dorada, espejo ardiente y vivo
con palomas suspensas en su vuelo,
feudo de terciopelo.
Paraíso nupcial, cielo cautivo.

Comarca de azucenas, patria pura
que mi mano recorre en un instante.
Mis labios en tu espejo palpitante
apuran manantiales de dulzura.

Isla para mis brazos nadadores,
santuario del suspiro:
Sobre tu territorio, amor, expiro
árbol estrangulado por las flores.

(De"Hombre planetario")

How many secret candles
under your skin!
Spheres painted by dawn!

Unique, live temple:
the divinity and the believer
ascend together in heaven.

VII

Your body is a garden, a bush of flowers
and animated rushes.
Domain of love that on its hills
I chase eternal splendors.

Golden water, flaming , live mirror
with pigeons stopped in midair,
realm of velvet,
nuptial paradise, imprisoned sky.

Residence of lilies, sacred patriotic territory
that my hand explores in an instant.
My lips in your palpitating mirror
urge springs of sweetness.

You are an island for my swimmer hands,
a sanctuary of sighs.
In your kingdom, love, I expire
like a tree choked by flowers.

CÉSAR MORO

BATALLA AL BORDE DE UNA CATARATA

Tener entre las manos largamente una sombra
De cara al sol
Tu recuerdo me persiga o me arrastre sin remedio
Sin salida sin freno sin refugio sin habla sin aire
El tiempo se transforma en casa de abandono
En cortes longitudinales de árboles donde tu imagen se
    disuelve en humo
El sabor más amargo que la historia del hombre conozca
El mortecino fulgor y la sombra
El abrir y cerrarse de puertas que conducen al dominio
    encantado de tu nombre
Donde todo perece
Un inmenso campo baldío de hierbas y de pedruscos
    interpretables
Una mano sobre una cabeza decapitada
Los pies
Tu frente
Tu espalda de diluvio
Tu vientre de aluvión un muslo de centellas
Una piedra que gira otra que se levanta y duerme en pie
Un caballo encantado un arbusto de piedra un lecho de piedra
Una boca de piedra y ese brillo que a veces me rodea
Para explicarme en letra muerta las prolongaciones misteriosas
        de tus manos que vuelven con el aspecto amenazante de
            un cuarto modesto con una cortina roja que se abre
                ante el infierno
Las sábanas el cielo de la noche
El sol el aire la lluvia el viento
Sólo el viento que trae tu nombre

(De ¨La tortuga ecuestre¨)

CESAR MORO
(Peru, 1903-1956)

BATTLE AT THE EDGE OF THE FALLS

To hold a shadow in your hands the longest time
Face to the sun
Pursued or dragged by your memory endlessly
Without exit uncontrollably without a word or a shelter,
    without air
Time is transformed in an abandonment
In longwise cuts of trees where your image
The most bitter taste ever known in the history of man merged
    with smoke
The death rattle majesty and the shadow
The opening and closing of doors leading to the enchanted
    reign of your name
Where everything withers away
An endless valley bare of grass and interpretable stones
A hand on a decapitated head
Your feet
Your brow
Your cataclysmic back
Your alluvial belly a thigh of sparks
A stone that rotates another stone and is elevated and sleeps
    standing up
A magical horse a petrified little tree a bed made of stone
A stone mouth and that brilliance that at times envelopes me
To explain to me in a dead writing the mysterious expansions
        of your hands that return with the menacing façade of an
            impoverished room with a red curtain that draws
                in front of hell
The bed sheets the night sky
The sun the air the rain the wind
Only the wind that bears your name

PABLO NERUDA

POEMA 15

Me gustas cuando callas porque estás como ausente
y me oyes desde lejos, y mi voz no te toca.
Parece que los ojos se te hubieran volado
y parece que un beso te cerrara la boca.

Como todas las cosas están llenas de mi alma
emerges de las cosas, llena del alma mía.
Mariposa de sueño, te pareces a mi alma,
y te pareces a la palabra melancolía.

Me gustas cuando callas y estás como distante.
Y estás como quejándote, mariposa en arrullo.
Y me oyes desde lejos, y mi voz no te alcanza:
déjame que me calle con el silencio tuyo.

Déjame que te hable también con tu silencio
claro como una lámpara, simple como un anillo.
Eres como la noche, callada y constelada.
Tu silencio es de estrella, tan lejano y sencillo.

Me gustas cuando callas porque estás como ausente.
Distante y dolorosa como si hubieras muerto.
Una palabra entonces, una sonrisa bastan.
Y estoy alegre, alegre de que no sea cierto.

PABLO NERUDA
(Chile, 1904-1973)

POEM 15

I like you when you are silent and you look as if you are
        absent,
and you hear me from afar, and my voice does not touch you.
You look as if your eyes are in flight
and it is as if a kiss has closed your mouth.

As all things take from my soul,
you emerge from everything filled of it.
Butterfly of sleep, you look like my soul,
and you look like the word melancholy.

I like you when you are silent and you look distant.
And you look as if you are a complaining butterfly in a cradle.
And you hear me from afar, and my voice does not reach you:
let me be silent with your silence.

Let me talk to you with your silence,
clear like a lamp, simple like a ring.
You are like the night, silent and constellated. Your silence
is simple like that of a very distant star.

I like you when you are silent and you look as if you are
        absent,
distant and anguished as if you have died.
One word then, a smile, is enough.
And I feel happy and joyful that it is not so.

POEMA 20   *a marisol*

Puedo escribir los versos más tristes esta noche.
Escribir, por ejemplo: "La noche está estrellada,
y tiritan, azules, los astros, a lo lejos".

El viento de la noche gira en el cielo y canta.

Puedo escribir los versos más tristes esta noche.
Yo la quise, y a veces ella también me quiso.

En las noches como ésta la tuve entre mis brazos.
La besé tantas veces bajo el cielo infinito.

Ella me quiso, a veces yo también la quería.
Cómo no haber amado sus grandes ojos fijos.

Puedo escribir los versos más tristes esta noche.
Pensar que no la tengo. Sentir que la he perdido.

Oír la noche inmensa, más inmensa sin ella.
Y el verso cae al alma como al pasto el rocío.

Qué importa que mi amor no pudiera guardarla.
La noche está estrellada y ella no está conmigo.

Eso es todo. A lo lejos alguien canta. A lo lejos.
Mi alma no se contenta con haberla perdido.

Como para acercarla mi mirada la busca.
Mi corazón la busca, y ella no está conmigo.

La misma noche que hace blanquear los mismos árboles.
Nosotros, los de entonces, ya no somos los mismos.

Ya no la quiero, es cierto, pero cuánto la quise.
Mi voz buscaba el viento para tocar su oído.

- cosa de la NOCHE
- Solidad
- tristeza
- melancoЛa
- obscuridad

147

POEM 20

I can write the saddest verses tonight.
Write, for instance: "The night is starry,
and the stars twinkle, azure, in the distance".

The night wind oscillates in the sky and sings.

I can write the saddest verses tonight.
I loved her, and at times she, too, loved me.

In nights like this I held her in my arms.
I kissed her many times under the infinite sky.

She once loved me, and there were times that I too, loved her.
How could I not have loved her big wide-open eyes.

I can write the saddest verses tonight.
To think that I have her no more. To feel that I have lost her.

Listen to the immense night, more immense without her.
And the verse falls on the soul like dew on the grass.

What does it matter that my love could not hold her.
The night is full of stars and she is not with me.

That is all. In the distance someone sings. In the distance.
My soul is sad for having lost her.

As if to get close to her my eyes are searching for her.
My heart looks for her, and she is not with me.

The same night whitening the same trees.
We, of that time, are not the same anymore.

I do not love her anymore, it is true, but how much I once
    loved her.
My voice searching the wind to touch her hearing.

De otro. Será de otro. Como antes de mis besos.
Su voz, su cuerpo claro. Sus ojos infinitos.

Ya no la quiero, es cierto, pero tal vez la quiero.
Es tan corto el amor, y es tan largo el olvido.

Porque en noches como ésta la tuve entre mis brazos ,
mi alma no se contenta con haberla perdido.

Aunque éste sea el último dolor que ella me causa,
y éstos sean los últimos versos que yo le escribo.

(De "Veinte poemas de amor y una canción desesperada")

SONETO IV

Recordarás aquella quebrada caprichosa
adonde los aromos palpitantes treparon,
de cuando en cuando un pájaro vestido
con agua y lentitud: traje de invierno.

Recordarás los dones de la tierra:
irascible fragancia, barro de oro,
hierbas del matorral, locas raíces,
sortílegas espinas como espadas.

Recordarás el ramo que trajiste,
ramo de sombra y agua con silencio,
ramo como una piedra con espuma.

Y aquella vez fue como nunca y siempre:
vamos allí donde no espera nada
y hallamos todo lo que está esperando.

(De "Cien sonetos de amor")

To another man. She will belong to another. Like before my
    kisses.
Her voice, her luminous body. Her infinite eyes.

I do not love her anymore, it is true, but perhaps I still do.
Love lasts only for a short time, forgetting takes longer.

Because in nights like this I held her in my arms,
my soul is sad for having lost her.

Even if this is the last pain she causes me,
and these the last verses I write for her.

SONNET IV

You will remember that strange precipice,
where the pulsating aromas came from,
and from time to time a bird dressed
in rain and sluggishness: the suit of winter.

You will again remember the gifts of the earth:
rushing fragrance and golden mud,
grass in the thicket, crazed roots,
magical thorns like long swords.

You will remember the wild flowers you gathered,
flowers of shadow, water and silence,
flowers like a foamy stone.

That time was like never or like always:
we go there where nothing is expected
and find all that is waiting to be found.

CARLOS OQUENDO DE AMAT

POEMA DEL MAR Y DE ELLA

Tu bondad pintó el canto de los pájaros

y el mar venía lleno en tus palabras
de puro blanca se abrirá aquella estrella
y ya no volarán nunca las dos golondrinas de tus cejas
el viento mueve las velas como flores
yo sé que tú estás esperándome detrás de la lluvia
y eres más que tu delantal y tu libro de letras
eres una sorpresa perenne

DENTRO DE LA ROSA DEL DIA

(De "Cinco metros de poemas")

CARLOS OQUENDO DE AMAT
(Peru, 1905 - Spain, 1936)

POEM OF THE SEA AND OF HER

Your kindness has painted the singing of the birds

and the sea was coming full of your words
that star will explode from so much whiteness
and the two swallows of your eyebrows will fly no more
the wind is waving the candles like flowers
I know you are waiting for me behind the rain
and that you are more than the school uniform and the book of
    letters
you are an eternal surprise

WITHIN THE ROSE OF THE DAY

AURELIO ARTURO

CANCION DE LA NOCHE CALLADA

En la noche balsámica, en la noche,
cuando suben las hojas hasta ser las estrellas,
oigo crecer las mujeres en la penumbra malva
y caer de sus párpados la sombra gota a gota.

Oigo engrosar sus brazos en las hondas penumbras
y podría oír el quebrarse de una espiga en el campo.

Una palabra canta en mi corazón, susurrante
hoja verde sin fin cayendo. En la noche balsámica,
cuando la sombra es el crecer desmesurado de los árboles,
me besa un largo sueño de viajes prodigiosos
y hay en mi corazón una gran luz de sol y maravilla.

En medio de una noche con rumor de floresta
como el ruido levísimo del caer de una estrella,
yo desperté en un sueño de espigas de oro trémulo
junto del cuerpo núbil de una mujer morena
y dulce, como a la orilla de un valle dormido.

Y en la noche de hojas y estrellas murmurantes,
yo amé un país y es de su limo oscuro
parva porción el corazón acerbo;

yo amé un país que me es una doncella,
un rumor hondo, un fluir sin fin, un árbol suave.

Yo amé un país y de él traje una estrella
que me es herida en el costado, y traje
un grito de mujer entre mi carne.

En la noche balsámica, noche joven y suave,
cuando las altas hojas ya son de luz, eternas…

AURELIO ARTURO
(Colombia, 1906-1974)

SONG OF THE SILENT NIGHT
In the balmy night, in the night,
when the leaves rise until they become stars,
I listen as women grow in the purple twilight
falling drop by drop from their eye lids.

I listen as their arms grow sturdy in the deep penumbra
and I would be able to hear the snapping of a wheat-stem in
      the valley.

A word is singing in my heart, green leaf murmuring
falling endlessly. In the balmy night,
when the shadow is an immense growing of the trees,
I am kissed by a long dream of magic travels
and my heart is flooded with the abundant light of sun and
      miracle.

In one night with whispers of blossoms
like the faintest sound of the fall of a star,
I woke up in a dream of tremulous golden wheat
next to the body of a sweet young brunette,
like in the edge of a sleeping valley.

And in the night of leaves and whispering stars,
I loved a country and the sour heart
is only a small portion of its dark mud.

I loved a country that for me is a woman,
a whisper, an endless flow, a tender tree.

I loved a country and from it I brought a star
which is a wound in the body, and I brought
the cry of a woman in my flesh.

In the balmy night, night sweet and young,
when the tall foliage is already light, eternal…

Mas si tu cuerpo es tierra donde la sombra crece,
si ya en tus ojos caen sin fin estrellas grandes,
¿qué encontraré en los valles que rizan alas breves?
¿qué lumbre buscaré sin días y sin noches?

MADRIGAL 3

No es para ti que, al fin, estas líneas escribo
en la página azul de este cielo nostálgico
como el viejo lamento del viento en el postigo
del día más floral entre los días idos.

Una palabra vuelve, pero no es tu palabra,
aunque fuera tu aliento que repite mi nombre,
sino mi boca húmeda de tus besos perdidos,
sino tus labios vivos en los míos, furtivos.

Y vuelve, cada siempre, entre el follaje alterno
de días y de noches, de soles y sombrías
estrellas repetidas, vuelve como el celaje
y su bandada quieta, veloz y sin fatiga.

No es para ti este canto que fulge de tus lágrimas,
no para ti este verso de melodías oscuras,
sino que entre mis manos tu temblor aún persiste
y en él el fuego eterno de nuestras horas mudas.

(De "Morada al Sur")

But if your body is earth where the shadow grows,
if in your eyes already big stars fall endlessly,
what will I find in valleys curled by tiny feathers?
For what light will I search endlessly without days or nights?

MADRIGAL 3

It is not for you, finally, that I write these lines
in the blue page of this nostalgic sky
like the old lament of the wind in the gate
of the day of blossoms of days gone by.

A word returns, but it is not your word,
even if it's your breath pronouncing my name,
but my mouth moist from your lost kisses,
your lips alive, fleeting, on mine.

And it returns, every always, in the foliage
of nights and days, of suns and dark reiterated stars,
it returns like the portent, and its tranquil flock
quick and infatigable.

This song gleaming from your tears, is not for you,
this poem of dark melodies, is not for you,
but in my hands your trembling persists
and in it the eternal flame of our silent hours.

ENRIQUE MOLINA

A VAHINE
(pintada por Gauguin)

Negra Vahíne
tu oscura trenza hacia tus pechos tibios
baja con su perfume de amapolas,
con su tallo que nutre la luz fosforescente,
y miras melancólica como el cielo te cubre
de antiguas hojas, cuyo rey es sólo
un soplo de la estación dormida en medio del viento,
donde yaces ahora, inmóvil como el cielo,
mientras sostienes una flor sin nombre,
un testimonio de la enloquecedora primavera en que moras.

¿Conservará la sombra de tus labios
el beso de Gauguin, como una terca gota de salmuera
corroyendo hasta el fondo de tu infierno
la inocencia -el obstinado y ciego afán de tu ser-;
ya errante en la centella de los muertos,
lejana criatura del océano…?

¿Dónde labra tu tumba
el ácido marino?
Oh Vahíne, ¿dónde existes
ya sólo como piedra sobre arenas azules,
como techo de paja batido por el trópico,
como una fruta, un cántaro, una seta
que pueblan los espíritus del fuego, picada por los pájaros,
pura en la antología de la muerte…?

ENRIQUE MOLINA
(Argentina, 1910-1996)

TO VAHINE
(painted by Gauguin)

Black Vahine
your dark braid descends
to your warm breasts perfumed by poppies,
whose stems are nourished by the radiant light,
and you look melancholy at the sky covering you
with ancient leaves, whose king is only
a breath of the season sleeping in the wind,
where you now lie, motionless like the sky,
holding a flower that has no name,
a testimony of the enchanting Spring where you dwell.

Will the shadow of your lips retain
Gauguin's kiss, like a persistent briny drop,
that erodes innocence to the depth of your hell
-the blind and persistent eagerness of your being-
already wandering in the spark of the dead,
remote creature of the ocean...?

Where is your tomb eroded
by the last salt of the sea?
Oh, Vahine, where do you exist now only
like a stone of blue shores,
like a weather-beaten thatch roof in the tropics,
like a fruit, or a jug, like a mushroom
where the spirits of fire reside pecked by the birds,
pure in the anthology of death...?

No una guirnalda de sonrisas
no un espejuelo de melosas luces,
sino una ley furiosa, una radiante ofensa al peso de los días
era lo que él buscaba, junto a tu piel,
junto a tus chatas fuentes de madera,
entre los grandes árboles,
cuando la soledad, la rebeldía,
azuzaban en su alma
la apasionada fuga de la cosas.
Porque ¿qué ansía un hombre
sino sobrepujar una costumbre llena de polvo y tedio?

Ahora, Vahíne, me contemplas sola,
a través de una niebla azotada por el vuelo de tantas
                invisibles aves muertas.
Y oyes mi vida que a tus pies se esparce
como una ola, un término de espuma
extrañamente lejos de tu orilla.

                (De "Pasiones terrestres")

It was not a garland of smiles
nor a mirage of mellowed lights,
but an enraged law, a thunderous attack in the passing of the
    days.
It was what he was seeking, next to your skin,
next to your wooden fountains,
amongst the tall trees,
when solitude and revolt
upset his soul,
the impassioned fleeing of things.
Because, what else can someone desire
if not to overcome a habit full of dust and boredom?

Now, Vahine, alone, you look at me,
from within the mist that whips
    the flight of so many dead birds.
And you hear my life scattered at your feet
like a wave, a rim of foam
strangely far from your shore.

MIGUEL HERNANDEZ

SONETO FINAL

Por desplumar arcángeles glaciales,
la nevada lilial de esbeltos dientes
es condenada al llanto de las fuentes
y al desconsuelo de los manantiales.

Por difundir su alma en los metales,
por dar el fuego al hierro sus orientes,
al dolor de los yunques inclementes
lo arrastran los herreros torrenciales.

Al doloroso trato de la espina,
al fatal desaliento de la rosa
y a la acción corrosiva de la muerte

arrojado me veo, y tanta ruina
no es por otra desgracia ni otra cosa
que por quererte y sólo por quererte.

(De "El rayo que no cesa")

MIGUEL HERNANDEZ
(Spain, 1910-1942)

FINAL SONNET

For plucking out the feathers of rigid archangels,
the tiniest flakes of lily white snow
are condemned to the sighing fountains
and to the despairing of the springs.

For defusing his soul in the metals,
for giving to the fire iron's splendor,
to the merciless anvils' ferocious pain,
he is dragged by torrential blacksmiths.

To the painful treatment of the crown of thorns,
to the fatal discouraging of the rose
and to the abolishing action of death

I am cast, and all this misfortune
is not destiny's persecution or another reason,
but because I have loved you, for this alone.

EMILIO ADOLFO WESTPHALEN

VINISTE A POSARTE...

Viniste a posarte sobre una hoja de mi cuerpo
gota dulce y pesada como el sol sobre nuestras vidas
trajiste olor de madera y ternura de tallo inclinándose
y alto velamen de mar recogiéndose en tu mirada
trajiste paso leve de alba al irse
y escandiado incienso de arboledas tremoladas en tus manos
bajaste de brisa en brisa como una ola asciende los días
y al fin eras el quedado manantial rodando las flores
o las playas encaminándose a una querella sin motivo
por decir si tu mano estuvo armoniosa en el tiempo
o si tu corazón era fruta de árbol o de ternura
o el estruendo callado del surtidor
o la voz baja de la dicha negándose y afirmándose
en cada diástole y sístole de permanencia y negación
viniste a posarte sobre mi copa
roja estrella y gorgorito completo
viniste a posarte como la noche llama a sus creaturas
o como el brazo termina su círculo y abarca el horario
        completo
o como la tempestad retira los velos de su frente
para mirar el mundo y no equivocar sus remos
al levantar los muros y cerrar las cuevas
has venido y no se me alcanza qué justeza equivocas
para estarte sin levedad de huida y gravitación de planeta
orlado de madreselvas en la astrología infantil
para estarte como la rosa hundida en los mares
o el barco anclado en nuestra conciencia
para estarte sin dar el alto a los minutos subiendo las jarcias

EMILIO ADOLFO WESTPHALEN
(Peru, 1911)

YOU CAME TO REST...

You came to rest on a leaf of my body
a drop sweet and heavy like the sun upon our life
you brought aromas of wood and the tenderness of a bent stem
and tall seafaring sails gathered in your glance
you brought a light pace of dawn when you left
and scanned incense of waving plantations in your hands
you descended from breeze to breeze as a wave ascends the
      days
and in the end you were the still fountain bordered by flowers
or the seashores driven to a needless quarrel
in order to say whether your hand was harmonious in time
or if your heart was the fruit of a tree or tenderness
or the abated noise of the fountain
or the low voice of fortune negating and assuring itself
in every dilation and contraction of permanence and denial
you came to rest on my foliage
incandescent star and full trill
you came to rest as night calls its creatures
or like the hour-hand closing its cycle within a full horary
or like the storm taking off the veils from her brow
to see the world and not mistake her oars
raising the walls and closing the caverns
you have come and it escapes me which accuracy you are
      mistaking
in order to be without the lightness of fleeing and the planet's
      gravitation
embroidered with honeysuckle in children's astrology
in order to be like the rose immersed in the sea
or the anchored ship in our consciousness
in order to be without stopping the minutes climbing the
      rigging

y cayéndose siempre antes de tocar el timbre que llama a la
    muerte
para estarte sitiada entre son de harpa y río de escaramuza
entre serpiente de aura y romero de edades
entre lengua de solsticio y labios de tardada morosidad
    acariciando
has venido como la muerte ha de llegar a nuestros labios
con la gozosa trasparencia de los días sin fanal
de los conciertos de hojas de otoño y aves de verano
con el contento de decir he llegado
que se ve en la primavera al poner sus primeras manos sobre
    las cosas
y anudar la cabellera de las ciudades
y dar vía libre a las aguas y canto libre a las bocas
de la muchacha al levantarse y del campo al recogerse
has venido pesada como el rocío sobre las flores del jarrón
has venido para borrar tu venida
estandarte de siglos clavado en nuestro pecho
has venido nariz de mármol
has venido ojos de diamante
has venido labios de oro

(De "Abolición de la muerte")

and falling always before you touch the alarm that calls death
in order to be under seige by the sound of the harp and the
    river of skirmishes
between the serpent of the breeze and the ageless rosemary
between the tongue of solstice and late slowness of caress
you came like death will come to our lips
with the pleasant transparency of days without lantern
of the concerts of autumn leaves and summer singing birds
with the satisfaction to say I have come
which is seen in the spring when it puts its early hands on
    things
to braid the hair of the cities
and give free access to the waters and song of the lips
of the girl getting up and the valley gathering itself
you have come heavy like the dew on the flowers in the vase
you have come to erase your arrival
banner of aeons nailed on our chest
you have come marble nose
you have come diamond eyes
you have come golden lips

OSCAR CERRUTO

EL AMOR

Como un vino de guerra la tarde
se nos brinda
y en lo alto canta la alondra.
¿Para qué más?
La alondra en lo alto
y aquí abajo dos copas
colmadas por un vino de guerra.
A qué inquirir sin causa
los números del cielo
si tu piel desafía
su imperio de amapolas
si en la azulada sombra
lecho de amor
tu labio solicita
el sello que devora.
Acerbo el aire pasa
sobre tu vientre sientes
su alado fuego y es mi mano
la que pulsa la dicha
y hace cantar el oro del verano.

(De "Estrella segregada")

OSCAR CERRUTO
(Bolivia, 1912-1981)

LOVE

The afternoon is offered to us
like a glass of war wine
and up, in heaven, the lark is singing.
What else to desire?
The lark in heaven
and down here, two glasses
overflowing with war wine.
Why should we investigate
the mysteries of heaven
if your skin disregards
its kingdom sown with poppies,
if in the blue shade,
-a bed of love-
your lips seek
the seal that devours?
The acrid wind is passing,
on your belly you feel
its winged fire and it is my hand
touching your delight
and makes the gold of Summer sing.

PABLO ANTONIO CUADRA

MANUSCRITO EN UNA BOTELLA

Yo había mirado los cocoteros y los tamarindos
y los mangos
las velas blancas secándose al sol
el humo del desayuno sobre el cielo
del amanecer
y los peces saltando en la atarraya
y una muchacha vestida de rojo
que bajaba a la playa y subía con el cántaro
y pasaba detrás de la arboleda
y aparecía y desaparecía
y durante mucho tiempo
yo no podía navegar sin esa imagen
de la muchacha vestida de rojo
y los cocoteros y los tamarindos y los mangos
me parecía que sólo existían
porque ella existía
y las velas blancas sólo eran blancas
cuando ella se reclinaba
con su vestido rojo y el humo era celeste
y felices los peces y los reflejos de los peces
y durante mucho tiempo quise escribir un poema
sobre esa muchacha vestida de rojo
y no encontraba el modo de describir
aquella extraña cosa que me fascinaba
y cuando se lo contaba a mis amigos se reían
pero cuando navegaba y volvía
siempre pasaba por la isla de la muchacha de vestido rojo
hasta que un día entré en la bahía de su isla
y eché el ancla y salté a tierra
y ahora escribo estas líneas y las lanzo a las olas en una botella

PABLO ANTONIO CUADRA
(Nicaragua, 1912)

MANUSCRIPT IN A BOTTLE

I had already looked at the coco-palms, the tamarinds
and the mangos
the white sails drying in the sun
the smoke of breakfast in the morning sky
and
the fish jumping in the nets
and a girl dressed in red who had gone down
to the shore and was returning with the bucket
passing behind the plantation
she appeared and disappeared
and for a long time
I could not steer the boat[1] without the image
of the young girl dressed in red.
The coco-palms and the tamarinds and the mangos
seemed to me that they existed only
because she existed
and the white sails were white only
when she half-reclined
with her red dress and the smoke was blue
and the fish happy and the reflections of the fish
and for a long while I tried to write a poem
for the girl who was dressed in red
and I couldn't find the way to describe
that strange enchantment
and when I related it to my friends they laughed
but when I was traveling in the lake on the return
I always passed by the island with the girl in the red dress
until one day I entered the little bay of her island.
I tied up my boat and I went ashore
and now I write these verses and I cast them in the waves in a
    bottle

[1] For many years Pablo Antonio Cuadra worked as a sailor in lake Nicaragua. Many of his poems are inspired by his experiences there. Here we find echoes from Greek Mythology, an allusion perhaps to Circe in the Odyssey. Translators' note.

porque ésta es mi historia
porque estoy mirando los cocoteros y los tamarindos
y los mangos
las velas blancas secándose al sol
y el humo del desayuno sobre el cielo
y pasa el tiempo
y esperamos y esperamos
y gruñimos
y no llega con las mazorcas
la muchacha vestida de rojo.

(De "Cantos de Cifar")

because this is my story
because I look at the coco-palms and the tamarinds
and the mangos
the white sails drying in the sun
the smoke of breakfast in the sky
and time goes on
and we wait and we wait
and we grunt
and the girl in red
does not appear with her basket of corncobs.

EDUARDO CARRANZA

AZUL DE TI

Pensar en ti es azul, como ir vagando
por un bosque dorado al mediodía:
nacen jardines en el habla mía
y con mis nubes por tus sueños ando.

Nos une y nos separa un aire blando,
una distancia de melancolía;
yo alzo los brazos de mi poesía,
azul de ti, dolido y esperando.

Es como un horizonte de violines
o un tibio sufrimiento de jazmines
pensar en ti, de azul temperamento.

El mundo se me vuelve cristalino,
y te miro, entre lámpara de trino,
azul domingo de mi pensamiento.

(De "Azul de ti")

EDUARDO CARRANZA
(Colombia, 1913-1985)

AZURE BECAUSE OF YOU

To think of you is blue as if strolling
in a golden forest at midday:
in my speech, gardens are born
and I go to my dreams with my clouds.

A gentle air unites and separates us,
a distance of melancholy;
then I raise my two hands of poetry,
azure because of you, sad.

To think of you is like a horizon
of violins or like a pain of jasmines:
to think of you in blue temperament.

The world changes to crystal for me,
and I watch you through a lamp of trills,
blue Sunday of my inner thoughts.

JOAQUIN PASOS

ESTA NO ES ELLA

Esta no es ella, es el viento,
es el aire que la llama;
es su lugar, es su hueco
vacío que la reclama.
Es sólo el aire que espera,
es la brisa que la aguarda,
pero no es ella, no es ella,
no es ella la que me habla;
es una luz en espejos,
es una sombra ocupada,
es el coche de su cuerpo.
¡Sólo es el coche que pasa!
Sólo es el árbol, la hoja
que la cubre y la acompaña,
es sólo su gesto que hunde
dedos de sueño en la nada.
Es el brazo que se abre,
es la mano que me llama,
pero no es ella, no es ella
aunque ésa sea su cara.
Esa es la cara del viento
ésa es la boca del aire,
esa bandada de besos
vuela dispersa y sin alas.
Para qué quiero este hueco
que le sirviera de almohada,
si a llenarlo ofrece el pecho
sólo un suspiro fantasma.
¿Para qué esta ausencia viva
que crece dentro del alma?
¿Para qué el aire, este aire
que con cara se disfraza?
Allí donde estaba un cuerpo
sólo un recuerdo se planta:

JOAQUIN PASOS
(Nicaragua, 1914-1947)

THIS IS NOT HER

This is not her, it is the wind,
it is the air calling her;
it is her place, it is her empty place
calling her back.
It is only the air that awaits her,
it is the wind that demands her
but it is not her, it is not her,
it is not her that speaks to me;
it is a light within mirrors,
it is an occupied shade,
it is the chariot of her body.
It is only the chariot going by!
It is only the tree, the leaf
that covers and accompanies her,
it is only her gesture that sinks
fingers of dreams into nothingness.
It is the opening of an arm,
it is the hand that calls me,
but it is not her, it is not her
although that is her face.
That is the face of the wind
that is the mouth of the air,
that embrace of kisses
flies scattered, wingless.
What do I want this empty hollow for
that served her as a pillow,
since in order to fill it the chest offers
only the ghost of a sigh.
What does this live absence
growing within the soul serve.
Of what benefit is the air, this air
masked to look like a face?
Where a body existed
there is only a memory:

y allí donde había voces,
cadáveres de palabras…
Hay una torre de iglesia
que ha perdido sus campanas,
hay una fuente en el monte
que se ha quedado sin agua;
cerca de un rosal sin rosas
nace un día sin mañana
y en este hueco del viento
donde estuviera entregada,
sólo un vacío desnudo
en forma de una muchacha.

(De "Poemas de un joven")

and where voices existed,
corpses of words...
There is a bell tower
that lost its bells,
there is a spring in the mountain
that went dry;
next to a rose-bush without roses
a day is born without morning
and in this hollow of the wind
where she was
there is only a naked emptiness
with the visage of a girl.

EDUARDO ANGUITA

EL VERDADERO MOMENTO

El pasajero al destello siente cruzar su halo
En el vacío lejanamente rumoroso
Y azul como si una piedra hubiera sido arrojada
Para turbar las ondas que dormían
Se dibuja la fronda de un encuentro.

Allí paseé con ella. Y con nosotros
Un aire de primavera nos seguía
Las hojas cantaban en la tarde
Jamás caería el sol y si se iba
Aún nos alumbraba.

Me cantaba Chansons Grecques de Ravel
Creo que a través de su rostro como a través de una hoja
Podía yo mirar el ocaso transparente
Y por su voz el tiempo se adelgazaba hasta la luz.

El fuego de la dulzura y el agua de los ojos
Eran notas en lo alto de los lejos
Por ellas podía yo descubrir el cielo
Hundir en él mi cabeza como en una madre.

Parece que el último instante fue frente al castaño
Cuando surgieron otro tiempo y otras personas
Pero lo que había ocurrido antes quedó para siempre
Lúcido y tranquilo como un estanque.

Hoy pasé por allí y por aquel instante
El momento y el lugar estaban muy lejos
Como en un grabado todo era más pequeño
Y ya no coincidían los objetos con sus imágenes.

EDUARDO ANGUITA
(Chile, 1914-1992)

THE REAL MOMENT

The passenger feels the sparks penetrate his halo
In the void of the distant sounds
And blue as if a stone was cast
To muddle the sleeping waves
The foliage of an encounter is sketched.

There I walked with her. And a Spring breeze
was following us
The leaves were singing in the afternoon
The sun would never set but if it had
It would still be illuminating us.

She was singing to me Ravel's Greek Songs.
I believe that in her face, as through a leaf
I would see the transparent sunset
And in her voice time stemmed to reach light.

The fire of the sweetness and the water of the eyes
were notes in ethereal heights.
Through her I could discover the sky and
Sink my head into it as in the arms of a mother.

It seems that the last moment was in front of the chestnut-tree,
When other people emerged and another time,
But what happened before remained for ever
Clear and calm like the water in a fountain.

Today I passed by there and in that minute
The moment and the place were very far away
As in an engraving, everything was smaller
And objects and their images did not coincide.

Comprendí que ella y yo ahora puestos al margen
De esa ella y de ese yo seríamos pesados
Con un peso de inexistencia de materia acumulada
Y que lo transparente de aquel pasado era lo único existente.

Ni el castaño ni yo ni ella ni la tarde semejantes
Ni la canción repetida frente al mismo jardín
Podríamos jamás coincidir con el verdadero MOMENTO:
Sólo superponernos condenados a fantasear
Como los concéntricos círculos de un estanque en que un torpe
Arroja piedras interminablemente.

(De "Poesía entera")

I understood that she and I were now redundant,
From her and from myself we would be weighed
On a scale of accumulated material non-existence
And only the transparency of that past existed.

Neither she nor I nor the chestnut-tree nor the afternoon were
the same, Not even the song that was repeated in front of the
    same garden
Could coincide again with the real MOMENT:
Only to superimpose ourselves condemned to fantasies.
Like the concentric circles of the water in a fountain
Where someone is always throwing stones.

OCTAVIO PAZ

PIEDRA DE SOL
(Fragmentos)
....
voy por tu cuerpo como por el mundo,
tu vientre es una plaza soleada,
tus pechos dos iglesias donde oficia
la sangre sus misterios paralelos,
mis miradas te cubren como yedra,
eres una ciudad que el mar asedia,
una muralla que la luz divide
en dos mitades de color durazno,
un paraje de sal, rocas y pájaros
bajo la ley del mediodía absorto,

vestida del color de mis deseos
como mi pensamiento vas desnuda,
voy por tus ojos como por el agua,
los tigres beben sueño en esos ojos,
el colibrí se quema en esas llamas,
voy por tu frente como por la luna,
como la nube por tu pensamiento,
voy por tu vientre como por tus sueños,

tu falda de maíz ondula y canta,
tu falda de cristal, tu falda de agua,
tus labios, tus cabellos, tus miradas,
toda la noche llueves, todo el día
abres mi pecho con tus dedos de agua,
cierras mis ojos con tu boca de agua,
sobre mis huesos llueves, en mi pecho
hunde raíces de agua un árbol líquido,

OCTAVIO PAZ
(Mexico, 1914-1998)

SUN STONE

(Excerpts)

....
I travel your body as I would travel the world,
your stomach is a sunlit square,
your breasts two churches where blood
officiates its parallel mysteries,
my glance wraps around you like ivy,
you are a city surrounded by the sea,
a wall fractured by the light
into two peach colored halves,
a domain of stones and birds
under the law of the profound noon,

clad in the colors of my desires
you walk naked like my thoughts,
I travel your eyes as I would travel the water,
tigers drink dreams in those eyes,
the humming bird burns in those flames,
I travel your forehead as I would travel the moon,
your thoughts, as a cloud,
I travel on your stomach as I would travel your dreams,

your skirt of corn flowers waves and sings,
your skirt of crystal, your skirt of water,
your lips, your hair, your eyes,
you rain all night, all day
you open my breast with your fingers of water ,
you close my eyes with your mouth of water,
you rain on my bones, inside my breast
a liquid tree sinks roots of water,

voy por tu talle como por un río,
voy por tu cuerpo como por un bosque,
como por un sendero en la montaña
que en un abismo brusco se termina,
voy por tus pensamientos afilados
y a la salida de tu blanca frente
mi sombra despeñada se destroza,
recojo mis fragmentos uno a uno
y prosigo sin cuerpo, busco a tientas,

. . . .
Madrid, 1937,
en la Plaza del Angel las mujeres
cosían y cantaban con sus hijos,
después sonó la alarma y hubo gritos,
casas arrodilladas en el polvo,
torres hendidas, frentes escupidas
y el huracán de los motores, fijo:
los dos se desnudaron y se amaron
por defender nuestra porción eterna,
nuestra ración de tiempo y paraíso,
tocar nuestra raíz y recobrarnos,
recobrar nuestra herencia arrebatada
por ladrones de vida hace mil siglos,
los dos se desnudaron y besaron
porque las desnudeces enlazadas
saltan el tiempo y son invulnerables,
nada las toca, vuelven al principio,
no hay tú ni yo, mañana, ayer ni nombres,
verdad de dos en sólo un cuerpo y alma,
oh ser total...

I travel around your waist as I would travel a river,
I travel about your body as I would travel through a forest,
a path in the mountain
that ends in a bottomless abyss,
I travel about your sharpened thoughts
and coming out of your white forehead
my shadow is wrecked and shattered,
I collect my fragments one by one
and continue on blindly, without body,

....
Madrid, 1937,
in the Plaza del Angel the women
were sewing and singing with their children,
then there was an air raid alarm and screams were heard,
homes kneeling into the dust,
bell-towers disemboweled, spat out facades
and the storm of the planes steady:
the two got undressed and made love
to defend our eternal share,
our share of time and Paradise,
roots to touch and revitalize ourselves,
to regain our inheritance captured
by the marauders of life thousands of aeons ago,
they got undressed and kissed each-other
because the entwined nudities
overcome time and are invulnerable,
nothing touches them, they return to the beginning,
there is no you nor me, tomorrow, yesterday, nor names,
the truth: two beings in one body and soul,
ah, being integral...!

....
todo se transfigura y es sagrado,
es el centro del mundo cada cuarto,
es la primera noche, el primer día,
el mundo nace cuando dos se besan,
gota de luz de entrañas transparentes
el cuarto como un fruto se entreabre
o estalla como un astro taciturno
y las leyes comidas de ratones,
las rejas de los bancos y las cárceles,
las rejas de papel, las alambradas,
los timbres y las púas y los pinchos,
el sermón monocorde de las armas,
el escorpión meloso y con bonete,
el tigre con chistera, presidente
del Club Vegetariano y la Cruz Roja,
el burro pedagogo, el cocodrilo
metido a redentor, padre de pueblos,
el Jefe, el tiburón, el arquitecto
del porvenir, el cerdo uniformado,
el hijo predilecto de la Iglesia
que se lava la negra dentadura
con el agua bendita y toma clases
de inglés y democracia, las paredes
invisibles, las máscaras podridas
que dividen al hombre de los hombres,
al hombre de sí mismo, se derrumban
por un instante inmenso y vislumbramos
nuestra unidad perdida, el desamparo
que es ser hombres, la gloria que es ser hombres
y compartir el pan, el sol, la muerte,
el olvidado asombro de estar vivos;
amar es combatir, si dos se besan
el mundo cambia, encarnan los deseos,
el pensamiento encarna, brotan alas
en las espaldas del esclavo, el mundo
es real y tangible, el vino es vino,
el pan vuelve a saber, el agua es agua,

....
all is transformed and is sacred,
every room is the center of the world,
it is the first night, the first day,
the world is born when two kiss,
drop of light of transparent viscera,
the room half opens like a fruit
or explodes like a silent star
and laws are chewed by mice,
the gates of banks and prisons,
the paper bars, the wire fences,
the car horns, the barbed wire, the thorns,
the single-chord sermon of the guns,
the mellowed scorpion with a crest,
the top-hatted tiger, President
of the Vegetarians' Club and the Red Cross,
the pedagogue donkey, the crocodile
dressed as a redeemer, father of the people,
the Chief, the shark, the architect
of the future, the uniformed pig,
the favorite son of the Church
washing his black denture
with holy water and attends classes
on democracy and English, the invisible
walls, the rotten masks
that separate man from men,
man from himself,
for an endless instant they fall and we glimpse
our lost unity, the abandonment
of being men, the glory of being men
able to share the daily bread, the sun and death,
the forgotten surprise of being alive;
to love is to fight, if two kiss
the world changes, desires incarnate,
the thought incarnates, wings sprout
on the shoulders of the slave, the world
is real, tangible, the wine is wine,
bread acquires taste, the water is water,

amar es combatir, es abrir puertas,
dejar de ser fantasma con un número
a perpetua cadena condenado
por un amo sin rostro;
                el mundo cambia
si dos se miran y se reconocen,
amar es desnudarse de los nombres:
………………..……………
(De "Piedra de sol")

NICANOR PARRA

CARTAS A UNA DESCONOCIDA

Cuando pasen los años, cuando pasen
Los años y el aire haya cavado un foso
Entre tu alma y la mía; cuando pasen los años
Y yo sólo sea un hombre que amó, un ser que se detuvo
Un instante frente a tus labios,
Un pobre hombre cansado de andar por los jardines,
¿Dónde estarás tú? ¡Dónde
Estarás, oh hija de mis besos!

(De "Poemas y antipoemas)

to love is to fight, to open doors,
to stop being a ghost with a number
condemned to life imprisonment
by a master without a face;
                              the world changes
if the two look at each other and recognize one another,
to love is to strip away names:
....

NICANOR PARRA
(Chile, 1914)

LETTERS TO AN UNKOWN WOMAN

When years go by, when
The years go by and the wind has dug a pit
Between our souls; when years go by
And I am nothing else but a man who loved,
Someone who stopped for a minute before your lips,
A poor man tired of walking the gardens,
Where will you be then? Where
Will you be, oh girl of my kisses!

GONZALO ROJAS

LAS HERMOSAS

Eléctricas, desnudas en el mármol ardiente que pasa de la piel
    a los vestidos,
turgentes, desafiantes, rápida la marea,
pisan el mundo, pisan la estrella de la suerte con sus finos
    tacones
y germinan, germinan como plantas silvestres en la calle,
y echan su aroma duro verdemente.

Cálidas impalpables del verano que zumba carnicero. Ni rosas
ni arcángeles: muchachas del país, adivinas
del hombre, y algo más que el calor centelleante,
algo más, algo más que estas ramas flexibles
que saben lo que saben como sabe la tierra.

Tan livianas, tan hondas, tan certeras las suaves. Cacería
de ojos azules y otras llamaradas urgentes en el baile
de las calles veloces. Hembras, hembras
en el oleaje ronco donde echamos las redes de los cinco
    sentidos
para sacar apenas el beso de la espuma.

GONZALO ROJAS
(Chile, 1917)

THE BEAUTIFUL ONES

Electrical, naked in the hot marble that filters from skin to
      clothes,
plump, defiant, rapid tide,
they step on the ground, they step on the star of fate with their
      delicate heels
and they sprout. They sprout like wild flowers in the street,
and in green color they disperse their fragrance.

Imperceptible summer fevers buzzing murder. Neither roses
nor archangels: local young girls, enchantresses
of the male, and something more than sparks of heat,
something more, something more than these willowy laughs
that know what they know as the earth does.

So ethereal, so profound, so sure the sweet ones,
A hunt by blue eyes and other urgent flames in the dance
of rapid roads. Females, females
in the hoarse waves where we cast our nets of the five senses
just to fish out a kiss from the foam.

¿QUÉ SE AMA CUANDO SE AMA?

¿Qué se ama cuando se ama, mi Dios: la luz terrible de la vida
o la luz de la muerte? ¿Qué se busca, qué se halla, qué
es eso: amor? ¿Quién es? ¿La mujer con su hondura, sus rosas,
    sus volcanes,
o este sol colorado que es mi sangre furiosa
cuando entro en ella hasta las últimas raíces?

¿O todo es un gran juego, Dios mío, y no hay mujer
ni hay hombre sino un solo cuerpo: el tuyo,
repartido en estrellas de hermosura, en partículas fugaces
de eternidad visible?

Me muero en esto, oh Dios, en esta guerra
de ir y venir entre ellas por las calles, de no poder amar
trescientas a la vez, porque estoy condenado siempre a una,
a esa una, a esa única que me diste en el viejo paraíso.

                          (De "Contra la muerte")

WHAT DO WE LOVE WHEN WE LOVE?

What do we love when we love, my God: the terrible light of
    life
or the light of death? What do we search for, what do we find,
    what
is this: love? Who is that? The woman with her depth, her
    roses, her volcanoes,
or this red sun that is my furious blood
when I enter her to the very last root?

Or all is naught but a game, my God, and there is no woman
nor man but only a body: yours,
divided into stars of beauty, in fleeting particles
of invisible eternity?

I'm dying, oh God, in this war
of coming and going among them in the streets and me,
unable to love three hundred at a time, for I'm condemned to
    one,
to just one, that unique one you gave me in the ancient
    Paradise.

MARIO FLORIAN

PASTORALA

Pastorala.
Pastorala.
Más hermosa que la luz de la nieve,
más que la luz del agua enamorada,
más que la luz bailando en los arco iris.
Pastorala.
Pastorala.

¿Qué labio de cuculí es más dulce,
qué lágrima de quena más mielada,
que tu canto que cae como la lluvia
pequeña, pequeñita, entre las flores?
Pastorala.
Pastorala.

¿Qué acento de trilla-taqui tan sentido,
qué gozo de wifala tan directo,
que descienda -amancay- a fondo de alma,
como baja a la mía tu recuerdo?
Pastorala.
Pastorala.

Yo le dije al gavilán ¡protégela!
Y a zorro y puma ¡guarden su manada!
(Y puma y gavilán y zorro nunca
volvieron a insinuar sus amenazas).
Pastorala.
Pastorala.

MARIO FLORIAN
(Peru, 1917)

PASTORA*

Pastora.
Pastora.
More beautiful than the light of the snow,
than the light of a running spring in love,
than the light radiating in the rainbows.
Pastora.
Pastora.

What lips of turtledove can be sweeter,
what tear of shepherd's flute more mellow
than your song falling in the flowers
like slender rain?
Pastora.
Pastora.

What tune of harvest song is more joyful,
what pleasure of a joyous cry can be closer,
descending-perfumed blossom- to the soul's depth,
as your memory drips into mine?
Pastora.
Pastora.

I call the falcon: guard her!
I told the fox and the puma: guard her flock!
(And the fox, the puma, and the falcon never
threaten her pack again).
Pastora.
Pastora.

Por mirar los jardines de tu manta,
por sostener el hilo de tu ovillo,
por oler las manzanas de tu cara,
por derretir tu olvido: ¡mis suspiros!
Pastorala.
Pastorala.

Por amansar tus ojos, tu sonrisa,
perdido, entre la luz de tu manada,
está mi corazón en forma de allco,
cuidándote, lamiéndote, llorándote…
Pastorala.
Pastorala.

(De "Urpi")

To look at the gardens of your mantle,
to hold the end of your spool's thread,
to smell the apples of your face,
to melt your forgetfulness: my sighs.
Pastora.
Pastora.

To soften your eyes and your smile,
lost, within the light of your flock,
my heart takes the form of a dog,
guarding you, licking you, mourning you...
Pastora.
Pastora.

----
* Shepherdess

IDEA VILARIÑO

YA NO

Ya no será
ya no
no viviremos juntos
no criaré a tu hijo
no coseré tu ropa
no te tendré de noche
no te besaré al irme
nunca sabrás quién fui
por qué me amaron otros.
No llegaré a saber
por qué ni cómo nunca
ni si era de verdad
lo que dijiste que era
ni quién fuiste
ni qué fui para ti
ni cómo hubiera sido
vivir juntos
querernos
esperarnos
estar.
Ya no soy más que yo
para siempre y tú
ya
no serás para mí
más que tú. Ya no estás
en un día futuro
no sabré dónde vives
con quién
ni si te acuerdas.
No me abrazarás nunca
como esa noche
nunca.
No volveré a tocarte.
No te veré morir.

(De "Poemas de amor")

IDEA VILARIÑO
(Uruguay, 1920)

NO MORE

It will not be
any more
we shall not live together
I will not raise your son
I will not sew your clothes
I will not have you at night
I will not kiss you when I leave
you will never learn who I was
nor why I was loved by other men.
I will never learn
why or how
or whether it was true
what you said it was
or who you were
or what I was for you
or how it would have been
living together
loving each-other
each waiting for the other
to be there.
I'm nothing else but me
for ever and you
you will not be
for me anything other than you.
You do not exist
in a day that will dawn
I will not know where you live
with whom
nor if you remember.
You will not take me in your arms
never again like that night
never.
I will not touch you again.
I will not see you die.

FERNANDO CHARRY LARA

TE HUBIERA AMADO

Te hubiera amado,
perfil solo, nube gris, nimbo del olvido.

Con el misterio de la mirada,
bajo la tormenta oscura de las palabras,
en la tristeza o puñal de cada beso,
hasta la ira y la melancolía,
te hubiera amado.

Ay, cuerpo que al amor se resiste
no ofreciendo su nocturno abandono a unos labios.
Sobre su piel la luna inútilmente llama,
llama inútil la noche
y el sol, inútil llama, lame
con una lengua sombría sus dos senos.

Te hubiera amado,
rostro donde el día toma su luz hermosa.
Frío, dolor, nube gris de siempre,
como un relámpago entre el sueño amanecías
sonámbula y bella atravesando
una aurora.

Tarde naval sobre el azul se extiende.
En el sueño del horizonte todo se olvida.
Vive tú aún, secreta existencia,
mía como el deseo que nunca se extingue.

Vive fuerte, relámpago que un día amanecías,
llama ahora de nieve.
Mírame aún, pero recuerda
que se olvida.

(De "Nocturnos y otros sueños")

FERNANDO CHARRY LARA
(Colombia, 1920)

I WOULD HAVE LOVED YOU

I would have loved you,
profile only, gray cloud, halo of forgetfulness.

With the mystery of vision
under the dark storm of words,
in the sadness and the stiletto of every kiss
to the fury of melancholy,
I would have loved you.

Oh, body that resists love
not offering your nocturnal abandonment to two lips.
The moon upon your skin calls uselessly,
night and sound call uselessly,
and the sun calls uselessly, licking
her two breasts with a dark tongue.

I would have loved you,
face from where day draws its beautiful light.
Cold, pain, the gray cloud of always,
like a lightning bolt in my sleep reaching the break of day
somnambulist and beautiful
crossing dawn.

A seaborn afternoon spreads over the blue.
In the dream of the horizon everything is forgotten.
Continue to live mystical being,
mine like the desire that never dissipates.

Live intensely, lightning bolt of dawn,
a flame of snow now.
Continue to look at me, but remember,
you can be forgotten.

OLGA OROZCO

NO HAY PUERTAS

Con arenas ardientes que labran una cifra de fuego sobre el
tiempo,
con una ley salvaje de animales que acechan el peligro desde
su madriguera, con el vértigo de mirar hacia arriba,
con tu amor que se enciende de pronto como una lámpara en
medio de la noche,
con pequeños fragmentos de un mundo consagrado para la
idolatría,
con la dulzura de dormir con toda tu piel cubriendo el costado
del miedo,
a la sombra del ocio que abría tiernamente un abanico de
praderas celestes,
hiciste día a día la soledad que tengo.

Mi soledad está hecha de ti.
Lleva tu nombre en su versión de piedra,
en un silencio tenso donde pueden sonar todas las melodías del
infierno;
camina junto a mí con tu paso vacío,
y tiene, como tú, esa mirada de mirar que me voy más lejos
cada vez,
hasta un fulgor de ayer que se disuelve en lágrimas, en nunca.

La dejaste a mis puertas como quien abandona la heredera de
un reino del que nadie sale y al que jamás se vuelve.
Y creció por sí sola,
alimentándose con esas hierbas que crecen en los bordes del
recuerdo
y que en las noches de tormenta producen espejismos
misteriosos,
escenas con que las fiebres alimentan sus mejores hogueras.

OLGA OROZCO
(Argentina, 1920)

THERE ARE NO DOORS

With the hot sand engraving a symbol of light upon time,
with a jungle law of beasts waylaying fear from their den,
 with the vertigo of looking up,
with your love which suddenly begins to flare like a candle in
 the night,
with small fragments of a world dedicated to idolatry,
with the sweetness of sleeping with all your skin covering the
 side of fear,
in the shade of idleness that opened tenderly a fan of celestial
 prairies,
day by day you created the solitude of my life.

My solitude is created by you.
Your name is on its stony facade,
in a taut silence where all songs of hell can echo;
it walks next to me with your empty place,
and like you, it has that look of seeing me getting farther and
 farther away,
up to a splendor of yesterday that dissolves in tears, into never.

You left it at my door like one who abandons the heir of a
 kingdom from where no one leaves and no one returns.
And it grew alone,
fed on that grass growing at the edge of memory
and which in stormy nights produces mysterious illusions,
scenes with which fevers nourish their greatest pyres.

La he visto así poblar las alamedas con los enmascarados que
    inmolan el amor
-personajes de un mármol invencible, ciego y absorto como la
    distancia-,
o desplegar en medio de una sala esa lluvia que cae junto al
    mar,
lejos, en otra parte,
dónde estarás llenando el cuenco de unos años con un agua de
    olvido.
Algunas veces sopla sobre mí con el viento del sur
un canto huracanado que se quiebra de pronto en un gemido en
    la garganta rota de la dicha,
o trata de borrar con un trozo de esperanza raída
ese adiós que escribiste con sangre de mis sueños en todos lo
    cristales
para que hiera todo cuanto miro.

Mi soledad es todo cuanto tengo de ti.
Aúlla con tu voz en todos los rincones.
Cuando la nombro con tu nombre
crece como una llaga en las tinieblas.

Y un atardecer levantó frente a mí
esa copa del cielo que tenía un color de álamos mojados y en
    la que hemos bebido el vino de eternidad de cada día,
y la rompió sin saber, para abrirse las venas,
para que tú nacieras como un dios de su espléndido duelo.
Y no pudo morir
y su mirada era la de una loca.

Entonces se abrió un muro
y entraste en este cuarto con una habitación que no tiene
    salidas
y en la que está sentado, contemplándome, en otra soledad
    semejante a mi vida.

                (De "Los juegos peligrosos")

I saw it inhabit the tree-lined alley with the masked people
    who sacrifice love
-heroes of an invincible marble, blind and absorbed like the
    distance-,
and unfold in a salon that rain that falls close to the sea,
far away, in another place,
where you will fill the hollow of the years with the water of
    oblivion.
Sometimes it blows on me with the South wind
a stormy song suddenly shattered in a cry in the throat of fate,
or tries to erase with a piece of stripped hope
that farewell you wrote with the blood of my dreams on all
    windows
so that it can lacerate all I see.

My solitude is all I have from you.
It howls with your voice in all the corners.
When I call it with your name
it grows like a wound in the darkness.

And one afternoon it raised before me
that celestial cup with the color of damp desolation from which
we drank the wine of
    everyday's eternity,
and broke it without knowing, to cut its wrists,
so that you will be born, a God from its splendid mourning.
And it could not die
and her look was that of a crazed woman.

Then a wall was opened
and you entered in this room, a home without doors
and here you stay, watching me, in another solitude like my
    life.

JAIME SAENZ

ANIVERSARIO DE UNA VISION

VII

Que sea larga tu permanencia bajo el fulgor de las estrellas,
    yo dejo en tus manos mi tiempo
    -el tiempo de la lluvia
    perfumará tu presencia resplandeciente
    en la vegetación.

Renuncio al júbilo, renuncio a ti: eres tú el cuerpo de mi alma:
    quédate
    -yo he transmontado el crepúsculo y la espesura,
    a la apacible luz de tus ojos
    y me interno en la tiniebla;
    a nadie mires,
    no abras la ventana. No te muevas:
    hazme saber el gesto que de tu boca
    difunde silenciosa la brisa;
    estoy en tu memoria, hazme saber si tus
    manos me acarician
    y si por ellas el follaje respira
    -hazme saber de la lluvia que cae sobre
    tu escondido cuerpo,
    y si la penumbra es quien lo esconde o el
    espíritu de la noche.

Hazme saber, perdida y desaparecida visión, qué era lo que
    guardaba tu mirar
    -si era el ansiado y secreto don,
    que mi vida esperó toda la vida a que la muerte
    lo recibiese.

(De "Aniversario de una visión")

JAIME SAENZ
(Bolivia, 1921-1986)

ANNIVERSARY OF A VISION

VII

Let your permanency under the brilliance of the stars be long,
    I leave my time in your hands
    -the time of rain
    will perfume your shining presence
    on the vegetation.

I resign from joy, I resign from you: you are the substance of
    my soul; stay
    - I have overcome the twilight and the forest,
    in the gentle light of your eyes
    and I lock myself in darkness;
    look at no one,
    do not open the window. Do not move:
    teach me the gesture with which your lips
    silently scatter the breeze;
    I am in your memory, tell me if
    your hands caress me
    and if the foliage is breathing through them
    -talk to me of the rain falling on
    your hidden body,
    and if it is the half light that hides it or the spirit
    of the night.

Let me know roving and lost vision, what was it that your
    glance guarded
    - if it were the desired and secret grace,
    that my life expected all its days
    to be taken by death.

JAVIER SOLOGUREN

OH AMOR ASOMBROSO

El amor asombroso
he aquí que se abren las tinieblas
centelleantes
he aquí el choque y el incendio
el furor más dulce
el fuego más tierno
he aquí las lenguas de la hoguera
buscándose trenzándose auscultándose
entre el fulgurante lecho de la noche
y el rocío de la aurora creciente
he aquí el olvido y el éxtasis
el instante con su sabor sin tiempo
la doble criatura que comulga
mutuamente devorándose
hela aquí por ti derribada
por ti crucificada
por ti resucitada

(De "Un trino en la ventana vacía")

JAVIER SOLOGUREN
(Peru, 1921)

OH, ASTONISHING LOVE

The astonishing love
here: it opens the spark filled darkness
here: I have the blaze and the clash
the sweetest violence
the tenderest fire
here: the tongues of flames
seeking   knotting   touching themselves
between the glowing bed of night
and the spreading dew of dawn
here: I have the oblivion and the ecstasy
the moment with the timeless taste
the double creature receiving communion
mutually devouring itself
here: I see it flung down by you
crucified by you
resurrected by you

JUAN SANCHEZ PELAEZ

RETRATO DE LA BELLA DESCONOCIDA

En todos los sitios, en todas las playas, estaré esperándote.
Vendrás eternamente altiva
Vendrás, lo sé, sin nostalgia, sin el feroz desencanto de los
    años
Vendrá el eclipse, la noche polar
Vendrás, te inclinas sobre mis cenizas, sobre las cenizas del
    tiempo perdido.
En todos los sitios, en todas la playas, eres la reina del
    universo.

¿Qué seré en el porvenir? Serás rico dice la noche irreal.
Bajo esa órbita de fuego caen las rosas manchadas del placer.
Sé que vendrás aunque no existas.
El porvenir: LOBO HELADO CON SU CORPIÑO DE
    DONCELLA MARITIMA.
Me empeño en descifrar este enigma de la infancia.
Mis amigos salen del oscuro firmamento
Mis amigos recluidos en una antigua prisión me hablan
Quiero en vano el corcel del mar, el girasol de tu risa
El demonio me visita en esta madriguera, mis amigos son
    puros e inermes.

Puedo detenerme como un fantasma, solicitar de mis
    antepasados que vengan en mi ayuda.
Pregunto: ¿Qué será de ti?
Trabajaré bajo el látigo del oro.
Ocultaré la imagen de la noche polar.

¿Por qué no llegas, fábula insomne?

(De "Elena y los elementos")

JUAN SANCHEZ PELAEZ
(Venezuela, 1922)

PORTRAIT OF THE BEATIFUL UNKNOWN WOMAN

In every place, on every shore, I will be waiting for you.
You will come eternally defiant
You will come, I know, without nostalgia, without the fierce
    disappointment of the years
The eclipse will come, the polar night
You will come, you will bend over my ashes, over the ashes of
    lost time.
In every place, on every shore you are the queen of infinity.

What will become of me? You will be wealthy the unreal night
    tells me.
Under this orbit of light fall the stained roses of delight.
I know that you will come, though you do not exist.
The future: A FROZEN WOLF WITH HIS MERMAID'S
    DOUBLET
I try to interpret this enigma of childhood.
My friends emerge from the dark firmament
My friends locked in an old prison talk to me
In vain I long for the charger of the sea, the sunflower of your
    laughter
The demon visits me in this burrow, my friends are pure, are
    defenseless.

I can be like a ghost, and ask my ancestors for help.
I ask: what will become of you?
I will work under the whip of gold.
I will hide the image of polar night.

Why don't you come, sleepless myth?

ALVARO MUTIS

HIJA ERES DE LOS LAGIDAS

Hija eres de los Lágidas.
Lo proclaman la submarina definición de tu rostro,
tu piel salpicada por el mar en las escolleras,
tu andar por la alcoba
llevando la desnudez como un manto que te fuera debido.
En tus manos también está esa señal de poder,
ese aire que las sirve y obedece
cuando defines las cosas
y les indicas su lugar en el mundo.
En un recodo de los años,
de nuevo, intacto,
sin haber rozado siquiera
las arenas del tiempo,
ese aroma que escoltaba tu juventud
y te señalaba ya como auténtica heredera
del linaje de los Lágidas.
Me pregunto cómo has hecho
para vencer el cotidiano uso
del tiempo y de la muerte.
Tal vez éste sea el signo cierto
de tu origen, de tu condición de heredera
del fugaz Reino del Delta.
Cuando mis brazos se alcen
para recibir a la muerte
tú estarás allí, de nuevo, intacta,
haciendo más fácil el tránsito,
porque así serás siempre,
porque hija eres del linaje de los Lágidas.

(De "Los emisarios")

ALVARO MUTIS
(Colombia, 1923)

YOU ARE A DAUGHTER OF THE LAGIDES

You are a daughter of the Lagides.
It is declared in the subaqueous definition of your face,
in your skin sprinkled by sea-water on the rocks,
your steps in the bedroom
wearing your nakedness like a mantle made for you.
But in your hands also there is that sign of authority,
that air which serves and obeys objects
as you define them
and mark their place in the world.
In a corner of the years,
again, intact,
without even having touched
the sandy shores of times,
that perfume which accompanied your youth
and was already marking you as the authentic heir
of the lineage of the Lagides.
I wonder how you managed
to defeat the everyday use of time
and death.
Maybe this is the true mark
of your ancestry, of your heiress' position
in the furtive kingdom of Delta.
When my arms are raised
to receive death
you will be there, again, intact,
making the passage easy,
because you will always be like that,
because you are a daughter of the lineage of the Lagides.

JORGE GAITAN DURAN

SE JUNTAN DESNUDOS

Dos cuerpos que se juntan desnudos
solos en la ciudad donde habitan los astros
inventan sin reposo el deseo.
No se ven cuando se aman, bellos
o atroces arden como dos mundos
que una vez cada mil años se cruzan en el cielo.
Sólo en la palabra, luna inútil, miramos
cómo nuestros cuerpos son cuando se abrazan,
se penetran, escupen, sangran, rocas que se destrozan,
estrellas enemigas, imperios que se afrentan.
Se acarician afímeros entre mil soles
que se despedazan, se besan hasta el fondo,
saltan como dos delfines blancos en el día,
pasan como un solo incendio por la noche.

(De "Amantes")

JORGE GAITAN DURAN
(Colombia, 1924 - French Antilles, 1962)

THEY UNITE NAKED

Two bodies that unite naked,
Alone in a city where stars dwell,
They invent desire unceasingly,
They don't look at one another when they make love,
Beautiful or horrid they are inflamed like two worlds
Meeting in the sky every one thousand years.
Only in the word, useless moon, we see
How our two bodies are when they embrace,
Unite, spit out, bleed, like rocks, being destroyed,
Stars hating one another, empires that affront each other.
They caress fleetingly within a thousand
Shattered suns, they kiss to the depths,
Leap like two white dolphins in the daylight,
Like a single flame they traverse the night.

Son criticos, ironicos
o sarcasticas
que terminan con
un verso sarastico.

216

ERNESTO CARDENAL

EPIGRAMAS

Te doy, Claudia, estos versos, porque tú eres su dueña.
Los he escrito sencillos para que tú los entiendas.
Son para ti solamente, pero si a ti no te intèresan,
un día se divulgarán tal vez por toda Hispanoamérica…
Y si al amor que los dictó, tú también lo desprecias,
otras soñarán con este amor que no fue para ellas.
Y tal vez verás, Claudia, que estos poemas,
(escritos para conquistarte a ti) despiertan
en otras parejas enamoradas que los lean
los besos que en ti no despertó el poeta.

*

De estos cines, Claudia, de estas fiestas,
de estas carreras de caballos,
no quedará nada para la posteridad
sino los versos de Ernesto Cardenal para Claudia (si acaso)
y el nombre de Claudia que yo puse en esos versos
y los de mis rivales, si es que yo decido rescatarlos
del olvido, y los incluyo también en mis versos
para ridiculizarlos.

*

Al perderte yo a ti tú y yo hemos perdido:
yo porque tú eras lo que yo más amaba
y tú porque yo era el que te amaba más.
Pero de nosotros dos tú pierdes más que yo:
porque yo podré amar a otras como te amaba a ti
pero a ti no te amarán como te amaba yo.

(De "Epigramas")

ERNESTO CARDENAL
(Nicaragua, 1925)

EPIGRAMS

I offer these verses to you, Claudia, because you are their
    mistress.
I wrote them simple so you can understand them.
They are for you alone but if they are not of interest to you
they may some day be known all over Latin America...
And if you also scorn the love that inspired them,
other women will dream this love which was not for them.
You may see then, Claudia, that these verses,
(written to conquer you) awake
in other couples, when they read them,
those kisses that the poet did not awake in you.

                 *

From those theaters, Claudia, from those feasts,
from those horse races,
nothing will remain for posterity
except the verses of Ernesto Cardenal for Claudia (perhaps)
and the name of Claudia that I put in these verses
and the names of my rivals, if I decide to put them,
to save them from oblivion and mention them here
in order to ridicule them.

                 *

For me to lose you and for you to lose me, we both lose:
I, because you were what I most loved
and you because I was the one who loved you most.
But of the two, you lose the most:
because I will be able to love others the way I loved you,
while you will never be loved by anyone the way I loved you.

CARLOS GERMAN BELLI

POEMA

Nuestro amor no está en nuestros respectivos
y castos genitales, nuestro amor
tampoco en nuestra boca, ni en las manos:
todo nuestro amor guárdase con pálpito
bajo la sangre pura de los ojos.
Mi amor, tu amor esperan que la muerte
se robe los huesos, el diente y la uña,
esperan que en el valle solamente
tus ojos y mis ojos queden juntos,
mirándose ya fuera de sus órbitas,
más bien como dos astros, como uno.

(De "Poemas")

CARLOS GERMAN BELLI
(Peru, 1927)

POEM

Our love is not found in our respective,
pure genitals, our love
is not found on the lips, nor in the hands:
all our love is guarded by heart beats
under the pure blood of the eyes.
My love, your love anticipate death
to take the bones, the tooth and the nail,
they anticipate that in the valley
only your eyes, my eyes will stay together,
looking at each other out of their orbits,
more like two stars or like one.

JUAN GONZALO ROSE

MARISEL

Yo recuerdo que tú eras
como la primavera trizada de las rosas,
o como las palabras que los niños musitan
sonriendo en sus sueños.

Yo recuerdo que tú eras
como el agua que beben silenciosos los ciegos,
o como la saliva de las aves
cuando el amor las tumba de gozo en los aleros.

En la última arena de la tarde tendías
agobiado de gracia tu cuerpo de gacela
y la noche arribaba a tu pecho desnudo
como aborda la luna los navíos de vela.

Y ahora, Marisel, la vida pasa
sin que ningún instante nos traiga la alegría…

Ha debido morirse con nosotros el tiempo,
o has debido quererme como yo te quería.

(De "Simple canción")

JUAN GONZALO ROSE
(Peru, 1928-1983)

MARISEL

I remember you were
like the scattered Spring of roses,
or like words the children whisper
laughing in their dreams.

I remember you were
like the water the blind drink silently,
or like the saliva of the birds
when love's desire throws them into the pediments.

In the last sand of afternoon you were stretching
your graceful body of antelope,
and night was reaching your bare breasts
the way the moon is boarding the sailing boats.

And now, Marisel, life goes by
without a minute of joy...

Time should have died with us then,
or you should have loved me as much as I loved you.

ENRIQUE LIHN

LA DESPEDIDA

¿Y qué será, Nathalie, de nosotros. Tú en mi memoria, yo en la
tuya como esos pobres amantes que mientras se buscaban
de una ciudad a otra, llegaron a morir
-complacencias del narrador omnividente, tristezas de su
ingenio- justo en la misma pieza de un hotel miserable
pero en distintas épocas del año?
Absurdo todo pensamiento, toda memoria prematura y
particularmente dudosa
cualquier lamentación en nuestro caso;
es por una deformación profesional que me permito este falso
aullido
ávido y cauteloso a un mismo tiempo. "Todo es triste- me
escribes- y confuso,
y yo quisiera olvidarlo todo". Pero te das incluso, entre
paréntesis
el lujo de cobrarme una pequeña deuda y la palabra adiós se
diría que suena
de un modo estrictamente razonable.

El amor no perdona a los que juegan con él. No tenemos
perdón del amor, Nathalie,
a pesar de tu tono razonable
y este último zumbido de la ironía, atrapada en sí misma,
como una cigarra por los niños.
El viento nos devuelve, a ti en Bonnieux,
a mí en un París que a cada instante rompe, contra toda
expectativa,
sus vagas relaciones lluviosas con el sol,
el peso exacto de nuestras palabras de las que hicimos un mal
gasto al cambiarlas por moneda liviana, pequeñísima,
y este negocio de vivir al día no era más que, a lo lejos, una
bonita fachada
con angustiados gitanos en la trastienda.

ENRIQUE LIHN
(Chile, 1929-1988)

FAREWELL

What will become of us, Nathalie. You in my memory, I in
        yours like those poor lovers seeking one another
from one city to the next and found death
-complacencies of the all seeing narrator, sadness of his
        intellect- in the same room of a poor hotel
but in different seasons of the year?
Every thought is absurd, every premature and particularly
        doubtful memory,
like whatever lament in our case;
it is because of professional malformation that I permit myself
        this false scream,
avid and cautious at the same time. "Everything is sad -you
write to me- and uncertain
and I would wish to forget all." But within the parenthesis you
        have
the luxury to collect a small debt and bidding farewell
totally reasonable.

Love does not allow us to play with it. Love will not forgive
        us, Nathalie,
the logical tone notwithstanding
and this last murmur of self-trapped irony,
like a cicada trapped by children.
The wind returns us, you to Bonnieux,
me to Paris, a city that at any minute breaks it off against all
        expectations,
its vague rainy relations with the sun,
the exact weight of our words that we wasted exchanging them
        with the light, small coins of little value,
and that tale to live from day to day, was no more than a nice
        pretense, a beautiful shop front with unhappy gypsies in
        the back.

El viento al que jugamos, Nathalie, mientras soplaba del lado
      de lo real, en la Camargue, nos devuelve
-extramuros de la memoria, allí donde el mar brilla por su
      ausencia
 y no hay modo de estar realmente desnudo-
palmerales roídos por la arena, el sibilino rumor de una
      desolación con ecos
de voces agrias que se confunden con las nuestras.
Es la canción de los gitanos, forzados
a un nuevo exilio por los caminos de Provenza
bajo ese sol del viento que se ríe a mandíbula batiente del
      verano y sus pequeños negocios.
Son historias también tristemente confusas. La diferencia está
      en que nosotros bajamos desde el primer momento el
      diapasón de la nuestra;
sí, gente civilizada… guardando, claro está, las debidas
      distancias
-mi desventaja, Nathalie- entre tu tribu y la mía.

Pero Lulú es testigo del Tarot; Lulú que parece haber nacido
      bajo todos los signos del zodíaco,
antes hada madrina que rigurosa vidente,
ella lo sabe todo a ciencia incierta, tu amiga.
Nada con los romanos y sus *res gestae:* el porvenir se lee bajo
      la inspiración
de los aerolitos, en la mano misma;
entre griegos no hay líneas decisivas: una muerte que dice,
      únicamente ella,
la última palabra de lo que un hombre fue; y el temblor en las
      manos, Nathalie,
el brillo o la humedad en los ojos, el deseo.
Lulú, Lulú, y éramos nosotros esos montes de Venus,
      viejecilla, tus huéspedes:
una amiga de toda la mitad de tu vida que se pegaba, otra vez,
      a tus faldas
en compañía de un silencioso, delirante extranjero.

Contra toda evidencia corroboro tus pronósticos:
ella y yo, querida, hicimos un largo viaje;

The wind we played with, Nathalie, as it blew from the side of
    the real in Camargue, returns us
-outside the walls of memory, where the sea shines with its
    absence
and there is no way to remain really naked-
palm-plantations eroded by the sand, the sybilline sounds of a
    desolation with echoes
of harsh voices merging with ours.
It is in the song of the gypsies -forced to a new exile in the
    roads of Provence under that sun of wind that laughs with
    the rattling denture of summer- and its small businesses.
They are stories also sad and confused. The difference is that
    we lowered since the very first moment the tone of our
    song;
yes, like civilized people…maintaining, of course, the right
    distance
-my disadvantage, Nathalie- between your tribe and mine.

But Loulou is the witness of the Tarot cards; Loulou who
    looks as if she were born under all the signs of the Zodiac,
fairy god-mother before she became a stern seer,
she, your friend, knows everything in an uncertain way.
Nothing with the Romans and their *res gestae;* the future is
    read under the inspiration of meteoric stones, in the hand;
Among Greeks there are no definite dividing lines: a death that
    names death only, the last word of what existed as human
    being and the trembling of the hands, Nathalie,
the shine or the dampness in the eyes, the desire.
Loulou, Loulou, and it was us those mountains of Venus, little
    old lady, your guests:
a friend of the entire half of your life who clung yet again, to
    your skirt, together with a silent, half crazy stranger.

Against every proof I verify your prophecies:
she and I, my love, made the long trip.

nos casamos en Santiago de Chile, fuimos espantosamente
    felices, sumamos nuestros hijos respectivos y aun nos
    quedó tiempo para reproducirnos con prodigalidad,
para volver a Bonnieux en compañía de tus nietos mucho más
    que legítimos.
Si nada de esto ocurrió, querida, demás está decir que lo
    tomarás tranquilamente,
digo mejor: metafísicamente.
Te habías limitado a constatar, lo sé muy bien, no la miseria de
    los hechos
sino los encantos de la verdad: ese temblor en las manos.
Tú eres más razonable que nosotros: existe una historia de lo
    que pudo ser "n'importe où hors du monde",
te mereces, Lulú, una cita de Baudelaire,
múltiples besos en las dos mejillas,
mi adiós a una Francia con la que te confundo, la única eterna
    ojalá, viejecilla.

Ah, nosotros en cambio... ni griegos ni romanos; gente dejada
    de sus propias manos, los que cambiamos el disco
    rápidamente
por temor a que los gritos llegaran al techo,
tránsfugas de la tribu en la tierra de nadie, calculadores,
    jugadores y tristes por añadidura. Y confusos.
Es por una deformación profesional que me permito, Nathalie,
    mojar estos originales
con lágrimas de cocodrilo frente al espejo, escribiéndote,
tratando de sortear la duplicidad del castigo.
En mi memoria, Nathalie, y en la tuya, allí nos
    desencontraremos para siempre
-el amor no perdona a los que juegan con él-
como si de pronto el espejo te devolviera mi imagen;
trataré de pensar que habrás envejecido.

(De "Poesía de paso")

We got married in Santiago de Chile, we were spontaneously
    happy, joined by our respective children and we still had
    time to multiply ourselves prodigiously,
in order to return to Bonnieux accompanied by your most
    legitimate grandchildren.
If nothing of all this happened, my dear, it's needless to say
    that you should take it with composure,
I mean: metaphorically.
You had limited yourself to verify -I know·it well- not the
    misery of the facts
but the enchantments of truth: that trembling of the hands.
You are more reasonable than us: there is a story of what could
    be "n'importe oú hors du monde,"
you deserve, Loulou, a visit from Baudelaire,
many kisses on both your cheeks,
my farewell to France which I identify with you, the only
    eternal one I wish to God, old girl.

Oh, we, on the contrary…neither Greeks nor Romans; people
    left to ourselves, we change rapidly the tune
lest our cries reach the sky,
deserters of the tribe in no man's land, opportunists, gamblers
    and on top of this sad. And confused.
It is because of professional deformation that I allow myself,
    Nathalie, to dampen the original of this writing
with crocodile tears in front of the mirror, as I write to you,
trying to figure out the duplicity of the punishment.
In my memory, Nathalie, and in yours, there we will lose trace
    of one-another for ever
-love does not forgive those who play with it-
as if suddenly the mirror returned my image to you;
I will try to imagine that you are now old.

JUAN GELMAN

UNA MUJER Y UN HOMBRE

Una mujer y un hombre llevados por la vida,
una mujer y un hombre cara a cara
habitan en la noche, desbordan por sus manos,
se oyen subir libres por la sombra,
sus cabezas descansan en una bella infancia
que ellos crearon juntos, plena de sol, de luz,
una mujer y un hombre atados por sus labios
llenan la noche lenta con toda su memoria,
una mujer y un hombre más bellos en el otro
ocupan su lugar en la tierra.

(De "Gotán")

JUAN GELMAN
(Argentina, 1930)

A MAN AND A WOMAN

A woman and a man carried along by life,
a woman and a man face to face
they dwell in the night, overflow through their hands
and they are heard rising free in the shadows,
their hands lean on the beautiful age of childhood
they have created, full of sun and light,
a woman and a man connected at the lips,
they flood the slow night with their memory,
a woman and a man the one more beautiful to the other,
they have their place on earth.

ROQUE DALTON

LA MEMORIA

Así eran las tardes de nuestra primera juventud
oíamos Las Hojas Muertas, My Foolish Heart
o Sin Palabras en el Hotel del Puerto
y tú tenías un nombre claro
que sonaba muy bien en voz baja
y yo creía en los dioses de mis antiguos padres
y te contaba dulces mentiras
sobre la vida en los lejanos países que visité.

En las noches de los sábados
dábamos largos paseos sobre la arena húmeda
descalzos tomados de la mano en un hondo silencio
que sólo interrumpían los pescadores en sus embarcaciones
        iluminadas
deseándonos a gritos felicidad.
Después regresábamos a la cabaña de Billy
y tomábamos una copa de cognac frente al fuego
sentados en la pequeña alfombra de Lurçat
y luego yo te besaba la cabellera suelta
y comenzaba a recorrer tu cuerpo con estas manos sabias
que nunca temblaron en el amor o en la batalla.

Tu desnudez surgía en la pequeña noche de la alcoba
del fuego entre las cosas de madera
como una flor extraña de todos los dones
siempre para llenarme de asombro
y llamarme a nuevos descubrimientos.

Y tu respiración eran dos ríos vecinos
y tu piel y mi piel dos territorios sin frontera
y yo en ti como la tormenta tocando la raíz de los volcanes
y tú para mí como el desfiladero llovido
para la luz del amanecer.

ROQUE DALTON
(El Salvador, 1935-1975)

MEMORY

This is what the afternoons of our first youth were like
we could hear the Dead Leaves, My Foolish Heart,
or Without Words in the Hotel of the Harbor
and you had a transparent name
that sounded beautiful in a low voice
and I believed in the gods of my ancient fathers
and I told you sweet lies
about life in the distant places I had visited.

On Saturday evenings
we took long walks on the sand
barefoot holding hands in deep silence
broken only by the fishermen in their lit boats
wishing us happiness.
Afterward we would return to Billy's hut
for a cognac in front of the fire
seated on the small Lurcat carpet
and then I would kiss your loose hair
and begin to run over your body with these knowledgeable
        hands
that never shake in battle or in love.

Your nudity would be revealed in the small night of the room
from the flame's reflection on the wooden furniture
like a strange flower that has all the graces
to always fill me with marvel
and invite me to new discoveries.

And your breath was two neighboring rivers
and your skin and my skin two borderless territories
and I inside you like the storm that touches the root of the
        volcanoes
and you for me the wet mountain path
leading to the light of dawn.

Y llegaba el momento en que eras sólo el mar
sólo el mar con sus peces y sus sales
para mi sed con sus rojos secretos coralinos
y yo te bebía con la generosidad del empequeñecido
otra vez el misterio de toda el agua junta
en el pequeño agujero abierto por el niño en la arena.

Ay amor y esta es la hora pocos años después
en que tu rostro comienza a hacerse débil
y mi memoria está cada vez más vacía de ti.

Tu nombre era pequeño y aparecía en una canción
de aquel tiempo.

(De "Los pequeños infiernos")

And there was a moment that you were only the sea
the sea alone with its fish and its salts
for my thirst with its red coral secrets
and I was drinking you in with the generosity of the one who
    shrunk
again in the mystery of all the waters concentrated
in the small hole the child dug in the sand.

Oh, love, and this is the hour a few years later
that your face begins to fade
and my memory of you empties more and more.

Your name was small and was
part of a song of that time.

JORGE TEILLIER

EN LA SECRETA CASA DE LA NOCHE

Cuando ella y yo nos ocultamos
en la secreta casa de la noche
a la hora en que los pescadores furtivos
reparan sus redes tras los matorrales,
aunque todas las estrellas cayeran
yo no tendría ningún deseo que pedirles.

Y no importa que el viento olvide mi nombre
y pase dando gritos burlones
como un campesino ebrio que vuelve de la feria,
ni que las madres cierren todas las puertas
porque ella y yo estamos ocultos
en la secreta casa de la noche.

Ella pasea por mi cuarto
como la sombra desnuda
de los manzanos en el muro,
y su cuerpo se enciende como un árbol de pascua
para una fiesta de ángeles perdidos.

El último tren pasa como un temporal
remeciendo las casas de madera,
las madres cierran todas las puertas
y los pescadores furtivos van a repletar sus redes
mientras ella y yo nos ocultamos
en la secreta casa de la noche.

(De "Poemas del País de Nunca Jamás")

JORGE TEILLIER
(Chile, 1935-1996)

IN THE SECRET HOUSE OF NIGHT

When she and I hid
in the secret house of night
at the hour when the transient fishermen
mend their nets behind the reeds,
even if all the stars fell to earth
I would not have asked them for a favor.

It does not matter that the wind forgets my name
and that it blows by with playful cries
like a drunk peasant returning from the fair,
or that the mothers close all doors
because she and I are hidden
in the secret house of night.

She walks in my room
like the naked shadows
of the apple-trees on the wall
and her body is set ablaze like a Christmas tree
for a feast of lost angels.

The last train goes by like a storm
shaking the wooden dwellings,
the mothers bar all doors
and the clandestine fishermen leave to take in their nets
while she and I are hiding
in the secret house of night.

ALEJANDRA PIZARNIK

SILENCIOS

silencio yo me uno al silencio
yo me he unido al silencio
y me dejo hacer
me dejo beber
me dejo decir

apuñalada por lo ausente
por la espera bastarda
renaceré a los juegos terribles
y lo recordaré todo

los náufragos detrás de la sombra
abrazaron a la que se suicidó
con el silencio de su sangre

la noche bebió vino
y bailó desnuda entre los huesos de la niebla

animal lanzado a su rastro más lejano
o muchacha desnuda sentada en el olvido
mientras su cabeza rota vaga llorando
en busca de un cuerpo más puro

luego
cuando se mueran
yo bailaré
perdida en la luz del vino
y el amante de medianoche

que hay
detrás de mis ojos
y de tus ojos
ahora que es de noche
en la sangre

ALEJANDRA PIZARNIK
(Argentina, 1936-1972)

SILENCES

silence I identify with silence
I have been connected with silence
I let myself be used
I let myself be drunk
I let myself say

stabbed by what is missing
by the disgraceful expectation
I will be reborn in the terrible games
and will remember everything

the shipwrecked behind the shadows
embraced the one who committed suicide
with the silence of blood

night drank wine
and danced naked amid the bones of the fog

animal flung to its most distant track
or naked girl seated within oblivion
while her gaping head wanders crying
searching for a purer body

afterwards
when they die
I will dance
lost in the light of wine
and the lover of midnight

who lives
behind my eyelids
and your eyes
now that night has fallen
in the blood

y no podemos ver
el mundo frío
grande

no importa si cuando llame el amor
yo estoy muerta
vendré
siempre vendré
si alguna vez
llama el amor

viajera de corazón de pájaro negro
tuya es la soledad a medianoche
tuyos los animales sabios que pueblan tu sueño
en espera de la palabra antigua
tuyo el amor y su sonido a viento roto

(De "El deseo de la palabra")

and we cannot see
the cold world
big

it does not matter that when love calls
I am dead
I will come
I will always return
if some day love will call

traveler of the heart of a black bird
yours is the midnight solitude
yours the animals that proliferate in your sleep
waiting for the ancient order
yours is the love and its sound of the cracked wind

EUGENIO MONTEJO

MARINA

Cuando tendida duermes a mi lado
y un tenue respirar mueve tu pecho,
me detengo a mirarte sobre el lecho
como a la orilla de un navío anclado.

Crece y decrece en ritmo sosegado
un oleaje de espumas al acecho,
mientras la noche borra a cada trecho
la nave, el muelle y el acantilado.

Sólo sé que es un barco lo que miro,
por quien mi vida ahora es menos corta
y su horizonte inmenso y sin muralla.

Un barco que a mi lado es un suspiro,
donde parto o regreso, no me importa,
porque siempre me lleva adonde vaya.

(De "El hacha de seda")
[Sonetos de Tomás Linden]

EUGENIO MONTEJO
(Venezuela, 1938)

MARINA

When you lie sleeping by my side
and a light breath moves your breast,
I sit and watch you on the bed
as on the deck of an anchored ship.

A benevolent wave of stalking foams
ebbs and gets stronger rhythmically,
while in each interval night erases
the ship, the precipice, the wharf.

I know that what I see is only a ship
from which my life now becomes longer
and her horizon is immense, free.

A ship which in my side is a sigh,
regardless if I'm leaving or if I'm returning,
because it always takes me wherever it goes.

JORGE DEBRAVO

LECHOS DE PURIFICACION

Los lechos son países deliciosos
donde sólo los seres elegidos
se pueden madurar. Desconocidos
se levantan de ellos los esposos

que los dioses protegen: silenciosos,
como después de ser purificados
con un agua divina; deslumbrados
como dulces terneros saludosos.

¡Ah, qué miedo me dan los que se alojan
en los lechos de amor y se remojan
en aguas de ternura hasta los huesos!

Qué miedo cuando surgen dulces, hondos,
transparentes y frescos hasta el fondo,
lavados con el agua de los besos…

(De "Devocionario del amor sexual")

JORGE DEBRAVO
(Costa Rica, 1938-1967)

BEDS OF PURIFICATION

Beds are countries of delight
where only the selected beings
can mature. The spouses,
unknown, arise from them

protected by the gods: silent,
as they would be after divine purification
with a holy water; illuminated
like two tender, healthy calves.

Oh, how terrified I am of those
who inhabit the beds of love and
get soaked to the bone with tender water.

What a fear when they emerge sweet,
profound, transparent and refreshed to their depths,
bathed in the holy water of kisses.

OSCAR HAHN

NINGUN LUGAR ESTA AQUI O ESTA AHI

Ningún lugar está aquí o está ahí
Todo lugar es proyectado desde adentro
Todo lugar es superpuesto en el espacio

Ahora estoy echando un lugar para afuera
estoy tratando de ponerlo encima de ahí
encima del espacio donde no estás
a ver si de tanto hacer fuerza si de tanto hacer fuerza
te apareces ahí sonriente otra vez

Aparécete ahí aparécete sin miedo
y desde afuera avanza hacia aquí
y haz harta fuerza harta fuerza
a ver si yo me aparezco otra vez si aparezco otra vez
si reaparecemos los dos tomados de la mano
en el espacio
               donde coinciden
                        todos nuestros lugares

OSCAR HAHN
(Chile, 1938)

NO PLACE IS HERE OR THERE

No place is here or there
All places are projected from within
All places are superposed on space

Now I project a place outward
I try to place it over there
above the space where you are not
to see whether after so much effort so much effort
you appear there smiling again

Come out come out there without fear
and from outside walk toward here
and try more, more
to see if I also appear again if I appear
if we both appear holding hands
in the space
                    where all
                              our places converge

CON PASION SIN COMPASION

La destrucción del ser amado por el ser amado
es una práctica común desde la antigüedad

Nos embestimos con pasión sin compasión
y dormimos aferrados a esos cuerpos exánimes

Al amanecer
nuestras cenizas aún lloraban abrazadas

Ahora busco tu amor
en todo resto que pasa por mi puerta

(De "Mal de amor")

WITH PASSION WITHOUT COMPASSION

The destruction of the beloved by the lover
is a common practice since ancient times

We lunge with passion and without compassion
and we sleep holding on to those breathless bodies

At dawn
our ashes were still crying together

Now I seek your love
in every relic passing by my door

DARIO JARAMILLO AGUDELO

ALGUN DIA

Algún día te escribiré un poema que no mencione el aire ni la
    noche;
un poema que omita los nombres de las flores, que no tenga
    jazmines o magnolias.
Algún día te escribiré un poema sin pájaros ni fuentes, un
    poema que eluda el mar
y que no mire a las estrellas.
Algún día te escribiré un poema que se limite a pasar los dedos
    por tu piel
y que convierta en palabras tu mirada.
Sin comparaciones, sin metáforas, algún día escribiré un
    poema que huela a ti,
un poema con el ritmo de tus pulsaciones, con la intensidad
    estrujada de tu abrazo.
Algún día te escribiré un poema, el canto de mi dicha.

(De "Poemas de amor")

DARIO JARAMILLO AGUDELO
(Colombia, 1947)

SOME DAY

Some day I will write a poem for you and I will not mention
    the air or the night;
a poem with no reference to names of flowers, with no
    jazmines or magnolias.
Some day I will write you a poem without birds or fountains,
    a poem that eludes the sea
and does not look to the stars.
Some day I will write you a poem that will just caress your
    skin
and change your glance to words.
Without comparisons without metaphores, some day I will
    write a poem that smells like you,
a poem with the rhythm of your pulse, with the crushing
    intensity of your embrace.
Some day I will write a poem for you, the song of my
    happiness.

CARLOS MONTEMAYOR

CITEREA

Oh Ella:
la bienevocada,
la de la furia y el arrepentimiento,
la ramera de dulzuras,
la más bella de todas las soledades
(oh Citerea: la diosa,
me lastima la dulzura,
me lastima cada resurrección, cada placer),
la desnuda, la quieta, la incesante,
la que despierta debilitada por el amor,
la sofocada, la sedienta sólo de sentir,
la de infinito lecho
                    e infinito recuerdo,
amada con furia y sin embargo intacta,
la efímeramente saciada y sin embargo eterna
como la espuma del mar,
la diosa de los muslos,
la diosa de la respiración
(oh mi tenacidad, mi conciencia),
la diosa de los dioses,
la puta,
Citerea,
oh Ella:
¿no ves que la danza me hiere la carne, los ojos, el
                    pensamiento?
Aturdido, lleno de placer,
como una flor que apenas el viento roba
despierto nuevamente ajeno a tu permanencia.
Oh Citerea, Citerea,
cuán dulce locura me despedaza y me hiere de palabras la
                    carne,
el desvanecimiento en que caigo y me duelo,
a solas, en el contacto,
en la fatiga de ser yo,
diosa,

CARLOS MONTEMAYOR
(Mexico, 1947)

CYTHEREA

Oh, she:
the well remembered,
she of the fury and repentance,
the hetera of sweetness,
the most beautiful of all solitudes
(oh, Cytherea: the goddess
the sweetness hurts me,
every resurrection hurts me, every pleasure),
the naked, the quiet, the incessant,
she, who awakes weak from love,
the suffocating, thirsty for sensual pleasure,
she of the infinite bed
      and infinite memory,
loved violently and yet intact,
the satiated ephemerously and yet eternal
like the foam of the sea,
the goddess of thighs,
the goddess of breath
(oh, my persistence, oh, my conscience),
the goddess of the gods,
the hetera,
Cytherea,
oh, she:
can't you see that the dance hurts my flesh, my eyes, my
                  thought?
Dazed, sensually satiated,
like a flower the wind is just stealing
I awake again a stranger to your permanency.
Oh, Cytherea, Cytherea,
such sweet madness tears and wounds my flesh with words,
the faint into which I sink and ache,
alone, in the contact,
in the fatigue of being me,
goddess,

cuán dolorosamente danzas en mi alma,
despintando su suelo con tus pies desnudos,
cruel como el alba,
como el sueño en que me hundo,
oh tú, la de dulce mención,
la dulcemente hallada,
la pura,
la que al desnudarse
con la mirada se viste,
oh Ella.

(De "Abril y otros poemas")

how sadly you dance in my soul,
blotting out its painted ground with your naked feet,
cruel like dawn,
like sleep into which I sink,
oh, you the sweet remembered,
the sweet found,
the pure,
the one who when she undresses
is dressed with the sight,
oh, She.

Bibliographical Notes

Agustini, Delmira. Montevideo, Uruguay, 1886-1914. In life and in literature, Delmira Agustini led a unique and rather obscure existence. Her enigmatic life ended in tragedy when her ex-husband killed her and then killed himself. In her short life, Agustini published **The White Book** (1907), **Songs of Tomorrow** (1910) and the **Empty Chalices** (1913), which was prefaced by Rubén Darío. In 1924 a collection of her work was published in two volumes.

Aldana, Francisco de. Alcántara (Cáceres), Spain, 1537 - Alcazarquivir, Morocco, 1578. Francisco de Aldana's adventurous character led him to the military as well as politics. He fought in Flanders and lost his life in the disaster of Alcazarquivir, as did Sebastián, the king of Portugal. His poems depict a man of love, heroics, and religious meditation. Although neglected and forgotten for a long time, Aldana was admired by writers such as Cervantes, Quevedo and Lope de Vega. His poems are contained in two volumes published in 1589/1591 and were well received by the critics of the Twentieth century, when he was finally re-discovered.

Anguita, Eduardo. Linares, Chile, 1914 - Santiago, 1992. Eduardo Anguita initially participated in the creationist movement of his compatriot Vicente Huidobro. Later his poetry became a personal philosophical concept of theology. In 1935 he collaborated with Volodia Teitelboim in the memorable **Anthology of New Chilean Poetry**. In 1994, his works were published posthumously in a volume entitled **Whole Poetry**.

Anonymous."**Romance of Love**" is one of the poems included in the anthology (cancionero) **Flor de Enamorados** published in Barcelona in 1562. Only one copy exists of this rare edition, and it is found in the Library of the University of Krakow. It was published again in 1954 by Antonio Rodríguez Monino and Daniel Devoto (Valencia, Editorial Castalia).

Anonymous. Cold Fountain, Cold Fountain. This anonymous writer is probably one of the best known of the Spanish tradition. His verse is a happy union between the symbolism of sensuality and the expression of finesse. This translation is from the excellent book of Dámaso Alonso **Medieval and Traditional Poetry** (1935 and 1942).

Arturo, Aurelio. Pasto, Colombia, 1906 - Bogota, 1974. Aurelio Arturo was an active attorney while publishing his poetry in newspapers and magazines, which was gathered in one anthology: **Residence in the South**, published in 1963. The small but unique collection is one of the most successful expressions of this country's literature. It has exercised "some sort of a magisterial secret" in Colombia's Letters. In 1973 he cooperated in the editorial committee of the prestigious literary magazine Echo.

Banchs, Enrique. Buenos Aires, Argentina, 1888 - 1968. Enrique Banchs' early poetry exhibits trends of late symbolism but his last work is an expression of finesse of the classical tradition and of the medieval Spanish troubadours. His best known collections are **The Boats** (1907), **The Rattle of the Falcon** (1909) and **The Urn** (1911). He led an active life in his country's literary endeavors as a member of the Writer's Union and the Argentine Academy of Letters.

Bécquer, Gustavo Adolfo (Gustavo Adolfo Domínguez Bastida). Seville, Spain, 1836 - Madrid, 1870. Gustavo Adolfo Bécquer's father, José Domínguez Bécquer was a well known painter who encouraged and influenced his children toward the arts. But Béquer showed very early where his preference lay; it was literature. In his short life he published the **History of the Temples of Spain** (1857). The **Rhymes,** which placed him among the greatest representatives of romanticism, was published in 1871. Also **Legends** and his journalistic chronicles were published posthumously.

Belli, Carlos Germán. Lima, Peru, 1927. Carlos Germán Belli's poetry is both bold and traditional, yet always within the realm of modern expression. Some of his collections are: **Poems** (1958), **Oh Cybernetic Fate** (1961), **The Foot on the Neck** (1964), **Sextinas and other Poems** (1970), **In Homage of the Nutritious Bite** (1979), **Wedding of the Pen and the Letter** (1985), **Action of Grace** (1992). Belli has been a member of the Peruvian Academy of the Language since 1982.

Cardenal, Ernesto. Granada, Nicaragua, 1925. Ernesto Cardenal studied literature at Columbia University in New York and the University of Mexico. At the age of 31, he became a novice in a United States trappist monastery and was ordained a priest in Colombia in 1965. He has served as Minister of Culture in the Sandinista Administration and has defended a poetic doctrine known as "exteriorism" which he practices. Cardenal's works include **Hour**

O (1960), **Epigrams** (1961), **Psalms** (1964), **The Doubtful Trait** (1966), **Homage to the American Indians** (1970), **Oracle in Managua** (1973), among others.

Carranza, Eduardo. Apiay (Llanos Orientales), Colombia, 1913 - Bogota, 1985. Eduardo Carranza was a central figure in the group "Stone and Sky", which was formed in Colombia in 1936, and inspired by the poetic discipline of Juan Ramón Jiménez. He was a member of the Colombian Academy of Letters. For a number of years, Carranza led a diplomatic career serving as cultural attaché in Chile and Spain. His poetic works include **Azure of You** (1920), **The Forgotten and the Alhambra** (1957), **To Speak While Dreaming and other Hallucinations** (1974), **The Sung Steps** (1975) and the volume **Carranza by Carranza**, published in 1985 by María Mercedes Carranza.

Carrera Andrade, Jorge. Quito, Ecuador, 1902-1978. For many years he worked as a diplomat in Spain, France, England, Japan and other countries. Some of the titles of his extensive poetic works are: **The Ineffable Pond** (1922), **Bulletin of Land and Sea** (1930), **Roll the Apple** (1935), **The Time of the Illuminated Windows** (1937), **Registry of the World** (1940), **Poetic Ages** (1922 - 1956 - 1958), **Planetary Man** (1963), etc. The book **The Evergreen Land** (1977) unites some of his interesting articles on the Colonial Period in Ecuador.

Casal, Julián de. La Havana, Cuba, 1863-1893. By profession, Julián de Casal was a journalist, where he distinguished himself as a refined social chronicler, literary and theatrical critic. His poetry and prose, influenced by French decadentism, are representative of the sensibilities of the turn of the century. His poetic work consists of three collections: **Leaves in the Wind** (1890), **Snow** (1892) and **Busts and Rhymes** (1893).

Cernuda, Luis. Seville, Spain, 1902 - Mexico City, 1963. Luis Cernuda studied at the University of Seville. In 1928 and 1929 he was a lecturer at the University of Toulouse and later in the Universities of Glasgow and Cambridge. He also served as a professor at Mount Holyoke College (USA). In 1952 he made his home in Mexico City, where he died in 1963. Among Cernuda's books are: **Profile of The Air** (1927), **Where Oblivion Dwells** (1934), **Like One Who Waits for the Dawn** (1936), **Desolation of the Chimaera** (1962). **Reality and Desire** (1936) is the most successful anthology of his work. He has also published a large number of critical essays.

Cerruto, Oscar. La Paz, Bolivia, 1912-1981. Oscar Cerruto started out as a journalist. In 1931 he joined the diplomatic service of his country and served in various places for many years. His first book **Alluvion of Fire** (1935) was a novel on the war of Chaco, but his more steady literary work was poetry, after the **Number of the Roses** (1957). Some of his poetic works include: **Captive Land of Salt** (1958) and **Segregated Star** (1975). The Institute of Ibero American Cooperation of Madrid published in 1985 the volume of his collective works, **Poetry**. Oscar Cerruto was a member of the Bolivian Academy of Language.

Cetina, Gutierre de. Spain, ca.1520 - Mexico ca.1557. Gutierre de Cetina was a soldier and poet who studied in Seville, where he received his classical education. He participated in military expeditions in Italy and Germany. Afterward, Cetina traveled to Mexico where he died a violent death. His poetry has been influenced by Ausiás March, Petrarch and other Italian poets. He also composed a considerable number of sonnets, songs and epistles, but his major work was the adaptation of the madrigal.

Cruz, Sor Juana Inés de la. (Juana de Asbaje y Ramírez). San Miguel Nepantla, Mexico, 1651 - Mexico City, 1695. In 1659, Sor Juana Inés de la Cruz became a nun in the Monastery of San Jerónimo, where she lived the rest of her life. She is a distinguished figure of Hispanic letters in which her poetic and prose works have no rival. Cruz's intellectual life was extraordinarily active since childhood, as recorded in her famous **Response to Sister Flor** (1691), a very important autobiographical text, which constitutes the first allegation of the defense of women's rights to knowledge and participation in the tasks of intelligence. She also wrote sacramental treatises and comedies. The first volume of her work entitled **Castalian Inundation of Dreams** appeared in 1689. The second volume (1692) includes the **First Dreams**, a capital work of baroque poetry.

Cuadra, Pablo Antonio. Managua, Nicaragua, 1912. Pablo Antonio Cuadra was initiated in the group "Avant Guard" and was editor of its magazine until 1931. He has participated and helped in the creation and direction of literary magazines in his country like: **The Fish and the Serpent**, among others. Cuadra has been a working journalist and his work in this field has also been influential.

His vast bibliography includes plays, essays and a prolific poetic production which includes **Nicaraguan Poems** (1934), **The Promised Land** (1942), **The Jaguar and the Moon** (1959), **Songs of Cifar** (1971), and **Seven Trees Against the Falling Evening** (1980) and others.

Charry Lara, Fernando. Bogota, Colombia, 1920. Fernando Charry Lara studied law in the National University in Bogotá, where he was the Director of its Culture Department since 1943. He collaborated with the literary magazines "Myth" and "Echo", two of the most influential in Colombia, with poems and essays. He is a member of the Colombian Academy of the Language. His rigorous poetic work has been included in many books such as **Nocturnes and other Dreams** (1949), **The Farewells** (1963) and **Thoughts of the Lover** (1981). **Flame of Live Love** (1980) includes all three. His critical essays, included in the collection **Reader of Poetry** (1975) and **Poetry and Colombian Poets** (1985) are as rigorous as his poetry.

Dalton, Roque. San Salvador, El Salvador, 1935 - 1975. Roque Dalton studied law in Chile and in his country, but he never finished his studies because of the existing political upheavals that drove him into exile, first in Mexico and then in Cuba, where he settled in 1962. In Cuba, Dalton published his essay **César Vallejo** (1963), his anthologies of poems **The Testimonies** (1964) and **Taverna and other Poems** (1969). In 1970 he published in Barcelona the **Small Infernos**. In 1975 he was executed by a dissident faction of the revolutionary organization to which he belonged. In 1986 an **Anthology of Texts on Roque Dalton** was published in Havana posthumously.

Darío, Rubén (Félix Rubén García Sarmiento). Metapa, Nicaragua, 1867 - León, Nicaragua, 1916. Rubén Darío was a decisive figure in the literary revolution of Spanish-American poetry at the end of the century. **Azure...**, published in 1888, is a milestone in the development of Modernism. **Profane Proses** (1896), **Songs of Life and Hope** (1905) and **The Wandering Song** (1907), are examples of his expression. Darío has written a considerable amount of prose and contributed much to the transformation of journalistic chronicle, literary criticism and short stories. On occasion, Darío accepted diplomatic missions in Spain and Latin America; but his main dedication was journalism.

Debravo, Jorge. Guayabo de Turrialba, Costa Rica, 1938 - San Jose, 1967. Jorge Debravo was a field worker in his childhood and adolescence and he spent the rest of his short life working for the Social Security Administration; both working experiences turned him into a "committed" poet. **Open Miracle** (1959) and **Devotionary of Sexual Love** (1974), are two of his books. **Major Anthology** (1974), includes a selection of his published and unpublished works.

Diego, Gerardo. Santander, Spain, 1896 - Madrid, 1987. Gerardo Diego studied piano and literature. He was a professor of literature and a critic of music, literature, cinema and arts. In 1948 he was elected a member of the Spanish Royal Academy of the Language. In his youth, Diego participated in the creationist and ultraist movements, but he never renounced his dedication to classical poetry and neo-gongorism, as proven by his famous **Poetic Anthology in Honor of Góngora** published in 1927. Diego's anthology **Human Verses** won the National Prize for Literature in 1925. Successive anthologies of his poetry were published in 1941, 1958, 1965, 1969 and 1970.

Florián, Mario. Cajamarca, Perú, 1917. The oral Inca tradition of poetic expression is evident in Mario Florián's work. He uses subjects and situations of the rural element and, at times, the language of native Indians. Some of the books which he considers characteristic of his work are: **Tune of Fauna** (1940), **Noval** (1943), **Turtledoves** (1944), **Songs of Ollantaytampu** (1966) and **Andean Elegy** (1977). He is a professor of history.

Gaitán Durán, Jorge. Pamplona, Colombia, 1924 - Point a Pitre, French Antilles, 1962. Jorge Gaitán Durán was a poet, essayist, and an extraordinary cultural animator. His literary magazine "Myth" (1955-1962) was an important projection in its time. He died in an airplane accident. His published works include: **Insistence in Sadness** (1946), **Presence of Man** (1947), **Astonishment** (1945), **Lovers** (1959) and **If I Wake Tomorrow** (1961).

García Lorca, Federico. Fuente Vaqueros (Granada), Spain, 1898 - Granada, 1936. Federico García Lorca is one of the most known and studied poets of the 1927 generation. Since 1919 he resided in Madrid, where he began his theatrical work in 1920. In 1921, he published his **Book of Poetry**. Lorca's production in this field was prolific and successful. His **Gypsy Songs (1928)** was a masterpiece of original Andalusian songs. His production of plays, which he treated as "dramatic poetry" were equally successful. The Spanish Civil War found him in Granada, where he was executed by the Franco nationalist forces.

Garcilaso de la Vega. Toledo, Spain, 1501 - Nice, France, 1536. Garcilaso de la Vega was an exemplary exponent of the Renaissance and an equally exemplary courtier in Charles V's palace, whose ideals - weapons and letters - he accomplished in full. He participated in military campaigns with the king, and he lost his life in one of them. His poetry, an expression of a new linguistic form, was influenced by the Italian poets. This new form is reflected in his works in terms of selection and naturalness of expression. His poems appeared for the first time in 1543, along with those of Juan Boscán. The most accomplished modern edition of his works, is that of Elias L. Rivers (Castalia, 1964, 1981).

Gelman, Juan. Buenos Aires, Argentina, 1930. Juan Gelman actively opposed the military dictatorships of Argentina in the seventies and his family suffered their brutality in its full force by the assassination of his son and his daughter in law. He lived in exile in Europe for 12 years working as a translator and journalist. When the dictatorship ended, he returned to Argentina, but after a short stay, he went to live in Mexico where he works as a journalist. "Laborious and tenacious interrogation of reality" has been said of his poetic work which started in 1956 with the selection **Violin and other Matters**. His many books that followed are true to this description. He enriches them with the application of various forms of composition and writing, such as intertextuality, heteronymia, elaboration of quotes, neologisms, etc. This is summed up in one of the most surprising adventures of actual Latin American literature, which one starts knowing in the books **Poetic Works** (1975), and **Interruptions I and II** (1988). In 1997, Juan Gelman was awarded the National prize for Poetry.

Gómez de Avellaneda, Gertrudis. Port of Prince (Camagüey), Cuba, 1814 - Seville, Spain, 1873. Gertrudis Gómez de Avellaneda lived in Spain since she was 22 years old, where she was an active participant in the literary scene and wrote many historical novels and romantic tragedies. Six volumes of her **Literary Works, Dramas and Poetry** were published in Madrid, between 1869 and 1871.

Góngora y Argote, Luis de. Córdoba, Spain, 1561-1627. Luis de Góngora y Argote was the son of Francisco de Argote, consultant and judge of goods confiscated by the Inquisition, and Leonor de Góngora, whose last name he added to his father's in 1582. He is the central figure of Spanish baroque, which was identified by his name. He practiced various forms of poetry with equal verbal dexterity: rondelets and romance, lyrical and burlesque poems, popular refrains, songs, sonnets, etc. His major poems **Fable of Polyphemus and Galatea** (1612) and **Solitudes** (1613), sowed the seeds of a cultural revolution of tremendous impact in the development of Spanish poetry. Dámaso Alonso's studies of Góngora's poetry provides the best understanding of his work.

Gutiérrez Nájera, Manuel. Mexico City, 1859-1895. At 16, Manuel Gutiérrez Nájera worked as a newspaper and magazine journalist. His writings exhibited an elegant style in the social and cultural chronicle which distinguished him. In his poetry and narrative Najera accomplished his goal to combine the French thinking with the Spanish form. With his writings he contributed to expand the scope to the new modernist currents. His **Fragile Short Stories** were published in 1883, and his **Poems** appeared posthumously in 1896.

Hahn, Oscar. Iquique, Chile,1938. Oscar Hahn is a professor of Spanish American literature at the University of Iowa. He has been for many years a coeditor of the **Handbook of Latin American Studies** of the Library of Congress in Washington. His books of poetry are: **Art of Dying** (1977), **Pain of Love** (1981), **Nuclear Images** (1983), **Fixed Stars in a White Sky** (1989), and **Stolen Verses** (1995). He is presently a corresponding member of the Chilean Academy of Language since 1991. He has also published important works on the **Fantastic Latin American Short Stories of 19th and 20th Centuries** and a collection of essays **Text on Top of Text** (1984).

Hernández, Miguel. Orihuela (Alicante), Spain, 1910 - Alicante, 1942. Miguel Hernández is one of the principal figures of contemporary Spanish literature; poet and playwright. Although as a child and adolescent he was a shepherd, he became a self-taught exceptional literary personality. His first book **Skillful in Moons** was published in 1933. In 1936 he published **The Incessant Ray**, his most important work. Hernández fought in the Spanish Civil War on the Republican side, and after a long illness he died in prison. His last works of great intensity published posthumously included: **Song and Romance, Writer of Absence,** and others.

Herrera, Fernando de. Seville, Spain, 1534-1597. Fernando de Herrera was a poet, scholar and the author of **Annotations on Garcilaso** (1580). Although he did not become an ordained priest, he was supported by the parish of his native city. A fact of principal importance in his life was his unfulfilled love for Leonore de Milán, wife of the Count of Gelves, in whose palace he participated in literary meetings. A year after the death of the countess, he published a selection of his work (1582). He also wrote epic poetry celebrating events and people of his time.

Herrera y Reissig, Julio. Montevideo, Uruguay, 1875-1910. Julio Herrera y Reissig was an important poetic figure in Latin America at the beginning of the century. His work is characterized by an imperative will to desecrate: the lucid, the ironic distance and the parody are of central importance in this audacious poetry, which does not pretend to reproduce reality but to contradict it as a pure verbal form. This resulted in the development of novel poetic ideas in Spanish America, something other poets saw before the critics did. Herrera y Reissig has written only one book: **The Pilgrims of Stone** (1910), published posthumously like the rest of his work.

Huidobro, Vicente. Santiago, Chile, 1893 - Cartagena (Valparaíso), 1948. Vicente Huidobro started his creationist doctrine with the plaquette **The Mirror of Water**, published in 1916. About that time he established himself in Paris where he collaborated with the avant-garde literary magazines North South and Dada. His books **Arctic Poems** and **Equatorial** were published in 1918 and **Altazor and Trembling of the Sky** were published in 1931. His work played an important role in influencing the poets in Spain and Latin America. "He is the invisible oxygen of our poetry" Octavio Paz has said. Not less important, though very little read, are his later read books of poetry and prose. **Huidobro: the Careers of a Poet** (1984) by René de Costa is an important book on his work.

Jaramillo Agudelo, Darío. Santa Rosa de Osos, Antioquia, Colombia, 1947. Darío Jaramillo Agudelo is a distinguished figure in Colombian Literature. He is one of its most active animators as an essayist, anthologist and director of cultural publications. His published poetic works are: **Stories** (1974), **Treatise of Rhetoric** (1978), **Love Poems** (1986), **From the Eye to the Language**, texts accompanying the engravings of the Colombian painter A. Roda (1995). His most recent novels are **Crossed Letters** (1995) and

Novel with a Ghost (1996). In 1987, D. Jaramillo Agudelo edited an anthology of Colombian love poetry with the suggestive title **Sentimentary**.

Jiménez, Juan Ramón. Moguer (Huelva), Spain, 1881 - San Juan, Puerto Rico, 1958.   Juan Ramón Jiménez's first poems were published in Madrid in 1898 and 1899. He was later connected with Rubén Darío and other modernist writers. **Platero and I** published in 1914 was a book of lyric prose which was extensively read in many editions. His initial poetic work was rich in symbolism, which he considered pure poetry. He influenced the Hispanic literature of the 20th century extensively. Jiménez was awarded the Nobel Prize for Literature in 1956.

Lihn, Enrique. Santiago, Chile, 1929 - 1988.   Enrique Lihn was one of the distinguished poets of his country. He studied design and painting in the School of Fine Arts in the University of Chile. He also collaborated with literary magazines and in 1965 he studied museum history in Europe with a grant from UNESCO. Lihn became a professor of literature in the Department of Human Studies of the University of Chile in 1972. Among his numerous publications are the following anthologies: **The Dark Room** (1963), **The Faint Music of Poor Spheres** (1969), **From Manhattan** (1979) and his impressive last book **Diary of Death**, published in 1989. His published work includes the novels: **The Orchestra of Crystal** (1976), **The Art of the Word** (1980); and short stories: **Rice-Water** (1964) and essays on literature and art.

López Velarde, Ramón. Jerez (Zacatecas), Mexico, 1888 - Mexico City, 1921.   Ramón López Velarde began studying law and started publishing his poems in provincial magazines and newspapers in 1908. In 1914 he moved to Mexico City, where he practiced law and taught literature. He published three books of poems: **The Devoted Blood** (1916) and **Anguish** (1919). **The Sound of the Heart** appeared after his death (1932). Velarde's unique writing, which stems from within the traditional system of expression, was decisive for the transformation and beginning of the new poetry in Mexico and in Latin America.

Lugones, Leopoldo. Rio Seco (Cordoba), Argentina, 1874 - Tigre Island (Buenos Aires), 1938.   Leopoldo Lugones was the major representative of modernism in Argentina. His cultural interests were encyclopedic (Literature, Science, Politics, History, Linguistics,

Religions) and were manifested in his work. **The Strange Forces** (1906), contains some of the most successful short stories of Latin American Literature of the Fantastic. In his poetry Lugones explored various thematic and stylistic options: the prophetic - visionary expression (**The Mountains of Gold**, 1897), the parnassian and symbolistic refinement (**The Twilight of the Garden**, 1905), ironic audacity and imaginative (**Lunario sentimental**, 1907), a record of people and affairs of the national reality (**Ancestral Poems**, 1928).

Machado, Antonio. Seville, Spain, 1875 - Collioure, France, 1939. For a number of years Antonio Machado taught French in Soria, Spain. Afterward, he studied philosophy and taught in Segovia, Spain from 1919. In 1927 he was elected member of the Royal Academy of Spain. Machado's poetic endeavors include: **Solitudes** (1903), **Solitudes, Galleries** and **Other Poems** (1907), **Fields of Castille** (1912), **New Songs** (1924), **The Land of Alvargonzalez and Songs of Alto Duero** (1938). He also wrote important critical essays which included Juan de Mairena (1936) and **The Complementary and other Posthumous Works of Prose** (1957).

Martí, José. La Havana, 1853 - Dos Rios, Cuba, 1895. José Martí was one of the principal figures in the political and literary history of Spanish America in the 19th century. His prose and verse combined the romantic vision of reality with the onset of the modernist period. Martí's biography and literary data, his views and thinking are enormous. **Little Ismael** (1882) and **Simple Verses** (1891) are the two books of verse published while José Martí was still alive. The **Free Verses** were published in 1913.

Medrano, Francisco de. Seville, Spain, 1570 - 1607. In 1584, Francisco de Medrano embraced the life of a monk with the Jesuits. Years later, in 1602, he left the monastery where he lived in Salamanca and spent his last years in Seville, the city of his birth, devoting all his time to writing poetry. His poems, all love sonnets, were published posthumously in Palermo by Pedro Venegas de Saavedra in a volume titled **Remedies of Love**. The life and work of Francisco de Medrano was studied and analyzed by the Spanish poet Dámaso Alonso, with the collaboration of Stephen Reckert and was published in 1958.

Mistral, Gabriela (Lucila Godoy Alcayaga). Vicuña, Chile, 1889 - Hempstead, New_York, 1957. Gabriela Mistral began her teaching career in 1905 which took her to various places in Chile. In 1922, she was invited by the government of Mexico to collaborate in the educational reforms proposed by José Vasconcelos, Secretary of Education. As a poet she became known in Chile when she was awarded the Literary Prize of the city of Santiago in 1914 for her Sonnets of Death. Her first book, **Desolation** was published in New York by the Spanish Institute (1922). It was followed by **Felling** (1938) and **Wine-Press** (1954). Gabriela Mistral served as Consul of Chile in Madrid, Lisbon, Petropolis (Brazil), Naples and California, and in 1945 she was awarded the Nobel Prize for Literature.

Molina Enrique. Buenos Aires, Argentina, 1910-1996. Enrique Molina was the principal exponent of surrealism in Argentina. His prolific literary influence was enriched by an exciting life and work experience: in his youth he sailed as a crew member in the Merchant Marine and traveled extensively. His poetry is a unique form in Latin American Literature: **The Things and the Delirium** (1941), **Terrestrial Passions** (1946), **Errant Customs or the Roundness of the Earth** (1951), **Antipodal Lovers** (1961), **Free Fire** (1962), **The Beautiful Furies** (1966), **The Last Suns** (1980), were among other books and personal anthologies. In 1973 Molina published an important novel: **One Shadow Where Doña Camila O'Gorman Dreams**.

Montejo, Eugenio. Caracas, Venezuela, 1938. Eugenio Montejo is a poet, author and essayist of exemplary and careful writing. **Absolute Tropic** (1982), **The Alphabet of the World** (1988) and **Goodbye to the 20th Century** (1992) are some of his books of poetry. His work **The White Workshop** (1983), is a book of essays on poets of the 20th century: K. Kavafis, A. Machado, Lucian Blaga, and others.

Montemayor, Carlos. Parral (Chihuahua), Mexico, 1947. Carlos Montemayor is a poet, essayist, and accomplished novelist and translator. He studied classical and modern languages and has made numerous translations from Greek, Latin and Portuguese into Spanish. His translations include the complete fragments of Sapho and, in collaboration with Rigas Kappatos, the **Anthology of Greek poetry of the 20th Century**. Montemayor is a member of the Mexican Academy of Language. As an essayist, he authored **The Lost Gods** (1979) and **Three Contemporaries** (1981). **April and other Seasons** (1989) is a collective book of his poetic works since 1977. **Memory of Summer** was published in 1990. One of his most recent novels is **War in Paradise** (1991) which was also published in English and French.

Moro, César. (Alfredo Quíspez Asín), Lima, Peru, 1903-1956. César Moro resided in France between 1925 and 1933 where he was influenced by the surrealist movement, whose aesthetic views he adopted. Upon his return to Peru and his consequent travel to Mexico, where he stayed for ten years, he materialized an intensive task as a poet and also as a painter, though his most significant work was his poetry. Most of his poems were written in French. The posthumous book **The Equestrian Tortoise** (1957) is a compilation of all his poems written in Spanish.

Mutis, Alvaro. Bogotá, Colombia, 1923. Poet and novelist, Alvaro Mutis studied in Brussels and in Bogota where he worked at various occupations specializing in commercial advertising. In 1956 he moved to Mexico, where he still resides. Mùtis' first poems were published in 1948: **The Balance** (in collaboration with Carlos Patiño), to be followed by **The Elements of Disaster** (1953), **The Lost Works** (1965), **Caravansaray** (1981), **The Emissaries** (1985), **An Homage and Seven Nocturns** (1987). In 1988 he published in Mexico the compilation of his works: **Sum of Magroll the Mast-Man**. In addition to his poetry, he is also known for his vast and fascinating work in prose. In 1974 he received the National Prize for Literature of Colombia, and in 1997 the Spanish literary prizes Prince of Asturias and Queen Sofia.

Navarrete, Fray Manuel de. Zamora (Michoacan), Mexico, 1768 - 1809. Fray Manuel de Navarrete's literary preference was neoclassicism. He remained faithful to that form of expression until the last stage of his work when he anticipated certain tones of preromantic sensibility. His poems on sacred and profane subjects **Poetic Entertainments** were published in 1873.

Neruda, Pablo. Parral, Chile, 1904 - Santiago, 1973. Pablo Neruda has been the 20th century's most influential poet of Latin America. The various stages of his poetry are marked· by books that are of capital importance in the process of Spanish language literature. Neruda's published work is included in: **Twenty Love Poems and a Song of Despair** (1924), **Residence on Earth** (1933 and 1935), **General Song** (1950), the various books of **Elementary Odes** (1954, 1956 and 1957), **Estravagaria** (1958), the five volumes of **Memorial of Isla Negra** (1964) and many posthumous publications. He was also well known for his political and public activity. In 1971 Pablo Neruda was awarded the Nobel Prize for Literature. The books of

Amado Alonso, Margarita Aguirre, Emir Rodríguez Monegal, Volodia Teitelboim, René de Costa and Hernán Loyola are excellent guides for the study of Neruda's poetry.

Nervo, Amado. Tepic (Nayarit), Mexico, 1870 - Montevideo, Uruguay, 1919. Amado Nervo studied theology; however, he did not continue for a degree. In 1894 he moved to Mexico city where he collaborated with Gutiérrez Najera's literary magazine Revista Azul. Years later, he collaborated with Revista Moderna. Those were the two most important Mexican publications of Modernism. In 1905 Amado Nervo became a diplomat. His literary activity was incessant, both in verse and in prose. Narratives, chronicles, essays, critiques, travel notes and poetry are included in a bibliography of 29 volumes of his **Complete Works** (Madrid, 1920-1928). He also published **Serenity** (1914) and in 1920 **The Immobile Beloved** was published posthumously as he wished.

Oquendo de Amat, Carlos. Puno, Peru, 1905 - Navacerrada, Spain, 1936. An almost legendary figure of Peruvian literature, Oquendo de Amat disappeared during the Spanish Civil War. His only book **Fifteen Feet of Poems** was published in 1927. It was written on a 15 foot single length of folding paper. In his poetry, the experimental inclination of the vanguard coexists with preferences of the native where the evocative expression coexists with a sentimental tone.

Orozco, Olga. Toay (La Pampa), Argentina, 1920.   Olga Orozco studied Philosophy and Letters at the University of Buenos Aires, and later joined the group of writers of the review Song. Her first book **From Afar** (1946), was followed by **The Dead Women** (1951), **The Dangerous Plays** (1962), **Savage Museum** (1974), **Songs to Berenice** (1977), **Mutations of Reality** (1979). Olga Orozco also wrote short stories, plays, criticism, and worked as a journalist. Some of the following anthologies of her poetic work helped make her well known: **Twenty Nine Poems** (Caracas, 1975), **Poetic Works** (1979) and **Pages of Olga Orozco Selected by Her** (1984), with an interesting preface by Cristina Piña.

Palés Matos, Luis. Guayama, Puerto Rico, 1898 - San Juan, 1959. In 1921, Luis Palés Matos founded the revolutionary poetic movement "Diepalism" with José I. De Diego Padró. With the publication of his book **Tuntún de Pasa y Grifería** (Trivialities of curly heads of hair and rings of hair, 1937), he manifested his orientation toward a poetry of Afro- Antillean expression and themes. This was an important stage of Matos' work, which also had other successful manifestations. **Poetry** (1957), contains almost all of his work since **Azalea** (1915).

Parra, Nicanor. San Fabian de Alico (Chillan), Chile, 1914.
Nicanor Parra studied mathematics at the University of Chile, and afterward he specialized in physics at Brown University and at Oxford. In 1937 he published the anthology **Without a Name.** One can see signs of his later work which was published in **Poems and Antipoems** in 1954, a book of extreme importance for modern Latin American Literature. His innovating proposal (in the conception of poetry and of the poem and the exploration of other expressive possibilities) was a radical view in itself; more so in **Salon Verses** (1962), **Artifacts** (1972) and **Sermons and Other Preachings of the Christ of Elqui** (1977 and 1979). In 1991 Nicanor Parra received Mexico's literary prize Juan Rulfo.

Pasos, Joaquín. Granada, Nicaragua, 1914 - Managua, 1947. Joaquín Pasos participated in the "Vanguard" group along with José Coronel Urtecho and Pablo Antonio Cuadra. He worked in various newspapers and became known for his humorous articles and satires of the dictator Somoza, for which he was imprisoned more than once. His poetic works, published posthumously, are gathered in the anthology **Brief Summing Up** (1947) and the volume **Poems of a Young Man** (1962), compiled by Ernesto Cardenal and published by Fondo de Cultura Económica of Mexico.

Paz, Octavio. Mixcoac, DF, Mexico, 1914 - 1998. Octavio Paz is one of the most significant contemporary writers of Latin America. He was awarded the Nobel Prize for Literature in 1990. Paz started his poetic work at the age of 19 **(Wild Moon)**. His work has been incessant and vigorous in poetry and in essays and also in memorable literary undertakings. **Freedom by the Word** (1949), **Sun - Stone** (1957), **The Violent Season** (1957), **Salamandra** (1962), **East Slope** (1969), **Turning Point** (1976), **Tree Within** (1987), and the selection **The Fire of Everyday** (1989) are some of his important books of poetry. **The Labyrinth of Solitude** (1950) and **The Arc and the Lyre** (1955), illustrate two directions of his provocative and fascinating essay-writing. His work in prose also includes: **Cross-Roads** (1965), **Post Datum** (1970), **Sons of the Mud** (1974), **Sor Juana Inés de la Cruz or the Pitfalls of Faith** (1982), **The Other Voice** (1990). Paz also founded and directed the leading influential literary magazines Plural (in stage 1971 - 1976) and Vuelta, "Turning Point" since 1976).

Pizarnik, Alejandra. Buenos Aires, Argentina, 1936 - 1972. Alejandra Pizarnik studied philosophy and literature at the University of Buenos Aires. From 1960 to 1964 she lived in Paris, where she worked in various publishing establishments. She translated the work of important writers like H. Michaux, A. Artaud and A. Cesaire into Spanish. Her poetry **The Most Strange Land** (1955), **The Last Innocence** (1956), **The Lost Adventures** (1958), **Tree of Artemis** (1962), **The Work and the Nights** (1965), **Extraction from the Stone of Madness** (1968), **The Musical Inferno** (1971), is characterized by intensity and expressive humility. After her suicide, the anthology of her prose and poetry **The Desire of the Word** (1975) and **Texts of Shadow and Last Poems** (1982) was published by Olga Orozco and Ana Becciu.

Quevedo y Villegas, Francisco Gómez de. Madrid, 1580 - Villanueva de los Infantes, Spain, 1645. Francisco Gómez de Quevedo y Villegas wrote poetry and prose and participated in important political activities of the Spain of his time. He was secretary of Philip IV since 1632, but because of his disagreements with the Count Duque de Olivares, he was imprisoned from 1639 to 1643. His prose is a mixture of political articles, ascetic, philosophical and moral; some festive and satirical and the famous picaresque novel **History of the Life of Buscón** (1626). His poems, which with those of Góngora and Lope de Vega are the utmost expression of lyricism of the 17th century, were published after his death. They include: **The Spanish Parnassus, Mountain Divided in Two Peaks** (1648) and **The three Muses Last Castalians** (1670). One of the best modern editions of his work is the one by José Manuel Blecua.

Rebolledo, Efrén. Actopan (Hidalgo), Mexico 1877 - Madrid, Spain, 1929. Efren Rebolledo was first published as a poet and prose-writer in the important Revista Moderna, founded in 1898. In 1907 he traveled to the orient, Norway and Spain as a representative of Mexico. An important characteristic of his poetry is the erotic preoccupation in his bold sonnets **Caro Victrix** (1916). Rebolledo was a famous translator of Oscar Wilde and Rudyard Kipling. His Complete Works appeared in 1968.

Rojas, Gonzalo. Lebu, Chile, 1917. Gonzalo Rojas worked as a professor of literature in the University of Concepción. Among his most important cultural accomplishments is the organization and direction of the National and International Meetings of Writers, which were held in the University of Conception in 1958, 1960 and 1962. The last meeting marked the big expansion of Latin American literature. Rojas' influential poetic work was first presented in 1948 with **The Misery of Man**. Some of his other principal books are **Against Death** (1964), **Dark** (1977), **From the Lightning** (1984), **Matter of Testament** (1988) and **The Beautiful Ones** (1991). In 1992, he was awarded the Prize for Poetry Queen Sophia, of Spain, and the National Prize for Literature in Chile.

Rose, Juan Gonzalo. Tacna, Peru, 1928 - Lima, 1983. Juan Gonzalo Rose's first book **The Armed Light,** appeared in Mexico in 1954 with a preface by León Felipe. The publications that followed marked various directions of his work. His intertextuality in **Report to the King and Other Secrets** (1969), where he sees texts and situations of history under a different light, wefe quite influential. His **Poetic Works** were published in 1974 with a preface by Alberto Escobar. By that time he had began writing the lyrics for songs, which became very popular in his country.

Ruiz, Juan, Archipreste de Hita. Spain, ca. 1295 - ca. 1353. Very little information can be traced to compile the biography of Juan Ruiz, the author of **The Book of Good Love**. What we know about him comes from the poem itself. He is supposed to have been sired by Alcala de Henares in some place in old Al-Andaluz. His book, which was preserved in three copies at the end of the 14th century, is a fundamental work of Spanish Literature. Its influence was instrumental not only in the development of poetry but also of prose, with the creation of heroes like Trotaconventos, which prefigures a Celestina and her future incarnations. There have been many interpretations of this singular treatise of love, but its extraordinary richness never ceases to fascinate and surprise the reader.

Saenz, Jaime. La Paz, Bolivia, 1921 - 1986. Jaime Saenz is a poet and prose-writer who developed his writing from the idea of seeing the poet as a mystic and alchemist. This idea underlines the visionary dimension and the engrossing tone of his work. Among Saenz's books of poetry are: **The Scalpel** (1955), **Death by Fact** (1957), **Anniversary of a Vision** (1960), **Profound Visitor** (1954), **The Cold** (1984). His novel **Felipe Delgado** ((1979) and the biographical and autobiographical narratives **Lives and Deaths** (1986), **The Magnet Stone** (1989) are in prose.

Sánchez Peláez, Juan. Altagracia de Orituco, Venezuela, 1922. Juan Sánchez Peláez lived in Chile, Paris and New York. His work of clear surrealist influence is one of the most innovating voices of Venezuelan poetry. Sánchez Peláez is the author of **Helen and the Elements** (1951), **Animal of Custom** (1959), **For which Cause or Nostalgia** (1981), among other books collected in the volume **Poetry**, published by Monte Avila (1993).

Silva, José Asunción. Bogota, Colombia, 1865 - 1896.   José Asunción Silva belonged to the elite class of his city. Very early he familiarized   himself with the European literary trends, especially decadentism and symbolism. His brief but forceful poetic works are sketchy due to his death at 31 by suicide. However, they herald expressive possibilities explored later by 20th century literature. He left an unpublished novel, **After Dinner**. His poetry was published posthumously.

Sologuren, Javier. Lima, Peru, 1921. Javier Sologuren is a poet, critic and translator.   His work, started in 1947, exists in the successive publications of **Continuous Life** (1966,1971,1979,1989), a title which perfectly fits his feverish dedication to this field. As a printer-publisher of the memorable Editions of "Rama Florida" Sologuren published more than 140 books of Peruvian, Spanish and Latin American authors and excellent translations. His writings on art and literature are collected in **Gravitations and Tangents** (1989). Javier Sologuren is a member of the Peruvian Academy of Language.

Storni, Alfonsina. Sala Capriasca, Switzerland, 1892 - Mar de Plata, Argentina, 1938. Alfonsina Storni was a poet and playwright. She worked as a teacher in Rosario, Argentina. She went to live in Buenos Aires in 1911 where she published her first poems in the review Caras y Caretas (Faces and Masks). In her work, Alfonsina Storni often expresses with clarity and boldness the social problem of prejudice against feminism.   Some of her books are: **The Sweet Damage** (1918), **Irremediably** (1919), **Languishment** (1920), **Ochre** (1925), **Death Mask and Trefoil** (1938). In Mar de Plata, Alfonsina Storni wrote her last sonnet: "I am going to die", which was published in Buenos Aires the day after her suicide.

Tassis y Peralta, Juan, Count of Villamediana. Lisbon, Portugal, 1582 - Madrid, Spain, 1622. Juan Tassis y Peralta was educated in the ambiance of the royal court. Although his family had the monopoly of the Post Office in Spain, Tassis was exiled for his political satires. His assassination gave way to legends of love affairs and vengeance. An admirer and defender of Góngora, he left an original lyrical work of rare intensity and perfection. His Works were published in Zaragoza, in 1629 and in Madrid in 1631.

Teillier, Jorge. Lautaro, Chile, 1935 - Valparaíso, 1996. Jorge Teillier studied history and worked for a while as a professor in his native city of Lautaro, Chile. When he moved to Santiago, he worked as an editor of the Bulletin of the University of Chile. With his first book **For Angels and Sparrows** (1956), he started a poetic current called "Poetry of Lars" (domestic gods) which had considerable influence in Chilean Literature. **Deaths and Marvels** (1971), includes all his work. **For a Ghost People** (1978), and **Letters for Queens of Other Springs** (1985) followed. His last book was an anthology: **The Lost Realms** (1993).

Terrazas, Francisco de. Mexico, 1525 - 1560. Francisco de Terrazas was the first poet born in New Spain. He was a son of a conquistador of the same name. In 1577 five sonnets were included in the manuscript of song anthology **Flowers of Various Poets**, compiled in Mexico City; in 1584 Cervantes praised him in the Song of Calliope of **The Galatea**. It is not known whether he traveled to Europe or if the closeness of his poetry to the Sevillian school is owing to a possible relation with Gutierre de Cetina, in Mexico. Although he wrote epic poetry, it was his lyric poems that gave him an important place in colonial literature.

Vallejo, César. Santiago de Chuco, Peru, 1892 - Paris, 1938. As has been pointed out by Alberto Escobar, Vallejo "personifies the process of poetry in Peru", and it should be added that in a great measure that of Latin America as well. **The Black Heralds** (1918), **Trilce** (1922) and the posthumous books **Human Poems and Spain, Let this Cup Pass from Me** (1939) illustrate, with singular intensity and precision, moments of radical changes that have occurred in the 20th century in the poetic trends and in the corresponding forms of expression. Profound studies on Vallejo have been published by A. Ferrari, A. Coyné, A. Escobar, J. Guzmán, R. Paoli, D. Sobrevilla, among others. Juan Larrea, the Spanish poet and friend of Vallejo is responsible for the publication of the important collective volumes **Aula Vallejo** in Cordoba, Argentina (1 - 12, 1959 - 1974).

Vega y Carpio, Lope Félix de. Madrid, Spain, 1562 - 1635. Lope Félix de Vega y Carpio studied in Alcala de Henares. He had a tumultuous love life despite his ordination as a priest in 1614. He has been the most prolific writer of Spanish Literature. As a playwright, he created the popular and national comedy and equally important is his vast poetic work, which includes romances, epistles, songs, eclogues, the epic-burlesque poem "The Gatomachy" and numerous sonnets whose first selection was **Human Rhymes** (1602). His prose includes **Arcadia, The Pilgrim in his Country** and **Dorothea,** among others.

Vilariño, Idea. Montevideo, Uruguay, 1920. Idea Vilariño is a professor of literature. She studied the works of Rubén Darío, Delmira Agustini, Julio Herrera y Reissig and the lyrics of the tangos. Her work on **Symmetric Groups in Poetry** was first published in 1958. Idea Vilariño started publishing poetry with the brief book **The Suppliants** (1945), and continued with numerous other books. Among them are **Nocturnes** (1955), **Love Poems** (1962), **Poor World** (1967), **No** (1980). She also compiled some important anthologies which have been published in Spain and in Cuba.

Westphalen, Emilio Adolfo. Lima, Peru, 1911. Emilio Adolfo Westphalen is a poet and essayist representative of the surrealist movement in Latin America. In 1933 he published **The Strange Islands** and in 1935 **Abolition of Death.** His critical works appearing in the literary magazines Las Moradas (1947 - 1949) and Amaru (1967-1971) are exemplary and very memorable. After many years of silence, his published and unpublished poetry was collected in one volume: **Another Crumbling Image** (1980).

PEDRO LASTRA (Chile, 1932). Poet, critic and professor of Literature. He studied at the University of Chile, where he also taught and conducted research from 1961 through 1972. Since 1972 he has been professor of Spanish-American Literature at the State University of New York at Stony Brook. In 1973, Lastra was named Honorary Professor of the University of San Marcos In Lima, Peru, and in 1996, he was awarded another honorary degree by the University of San Andres in La Paz, Bolivia. Since 1978, he has been editor of Latin-American poetry for the Handbook of Latin American Studies published by the Library of Congress in Washington, DC.

As a critic and editor he has written works on Colonial Literature, 19th century Spanish-American Literature and studies on contemporary authors like: Gabriel García Márquez, Julio Cortázar, Enrique Lihn, Oscar Hahn and other Latin-American writers and poets. His books of poetry have been published in Chile, Peru, Mexico and the United States. Between 1966 and 1973, he was literary assistant of the University of Chile Publishing House where he founded and directed the collection "Letters of America".

Pedro Lastra is a corresponding member of the Chilean Academy of Language and, since 1995, Professor Emeritus of the State University of New York at Stony Brook.

RIGAS KAPPATOS (Cephalonia, Greece, 1934). Poet, short story writer, anthologist and translator. He worked for many years in the Greek Merchant Marine. In 1969 he settled in New York where he now lives but he frequently visits his country of birth where most of his books are published.

He studied literature, music and foreign languages, but his central activity as translator is related with Spanish, concentrating mainly in Latin-American Literature. His work in this field is summed up in ten books of poetry, short stories and essays, and includes the complete poetic works of Federico García Lorca (in collaboration with the novelist Kosmas Politis), and César Vallejo, selections from the work of Pablo Neruda and Nicanor Parra, anthologies of Latin American poetry, and of·Peruvian and Chilean short stories (the last two in collaboration with the poets Javier Sologuren and Pedro Lastra, respectively). In 1995 his translation of the Dictionary of Symbols, by Juan Eduardo Cirlot was published in Athens and in 1996 the anthology of prose and poetic works compiled in the volume The Cat in World Literature, a publication accompanied with illustrations of paintings and pictures concerning the cat in the world of arts.

He has also been collaborating for many years with literary magazines in Athens and with the Greek daily Proini of New York, where he writes reviews on books, literary articles and presents Latin-American writers through commentaries, translations and interviews.

In collaboration with the Mexican poet and novelist Carlos Montemayor, Rigas Kappatos has published in Spanish, in Mexico, his book The Poems of Athinulis and Anthology of Contemporary Greek Poetry. Six books of his own poetry have been published in Athens; a book of his short stories about animals, will appear soon.

ELENI PAIDOUSSI was born in Washington D. C. and is the author of eleven books of poetry and prose written in English and Greek. She obtained a BA from Queens College and a Masters Degree from St. John's University. Eleni Paidoussi is presently a teacher in the New York City School System.

RENE DE COSTA (1939) is an American of Greek descent who, after graduating from Rutgers University in 1964, taught mathematics in Colombia, South America. It was there, at the beginning of the "boom," that his interest in literature was kindled, and he returned to the United States to do a doctorate in Spanish American literature at Washington University in Saint Louis. He has been at the University of Chicago since 1970 and has served as Director of its Center for Latin American Studies.

His principal area of research and publication concerns the painting and poetry of the early twentieth-century avant-garde in France, Spain and Latin America. Professor de Costa is best known for The Poetry of Pablo Neruda (Harvard, 1979) and Vicente Huidobro: the Careers of a Poet (Oxford, 1984). His latest book, soon to be published in Spain and the United States is on the subject of Humor in Borges. He has also organized exhibitions in Madrid, Paris and Chicago on the interrelationship of literature and the plastic arts in the work of Juan Gris (1985), Vicente Huidobro (1987), and the visual poetry of Nicanor Parra and Joan Brossa (1992).

Since he likes to cook, he has most recently shared his expertise in a practical handbook titled La cocina varonil, the "macho" cookbook.